Climate Change and the Blue Economy: Supporting Marine Protected Areas While Advancing Biodiversity Conservation, Ocean Resilience, Sustainable Fisheries, and Ecotourism

Copyright

Climate Change and the Blue Economy: Supporting Marine Protected Areas While Advancing Biodiversity Conservation, Ocean Resilience, Sustainable Fisheries, and Ecotourism

© 2025 Robert C. Brears

ISBN (eBook): 978-1-991368-27-0

ISBN (Paperback): 978-1-991368-28-7

Published by Global Climate Solutions

First Edition, 2025

Cover design and interior layout by Global Climate Solutions

Table of Contents

Introduction

The oceans are at the heart of life on Earth. They regulate the planet's climate, provide oxygen, sustain vast ecosystems, and support billions of people through food, jobs, and cultural identity. As global pressures intensify—ranging from overfishing and pollution to climate change and habitat loss—the need for a balanced approach to ocean management has never been greater. The concept of the Blue Economy has emerged in response, offering a framework that promotes sustainable use of marine resources for economic growth, improved livelihoods, and healthy ecosystems. Rather than viewing the oceans purely as a source of extractive wealth, the Blue Economy emphasizes stewardship, resilience, and intergenerational responsibility.

At the center of this vision are Marine Protected Areas (MPAs). These designated zones safeguard ecosystems by limiting harmful activities, conserving biodiversity, and ensuring that marine habitats remain productive and resilient. MPAs are not just about conservation; they are also vital enablers of sustainable development. By protecting spawning grounds and key habitats, they support fish populations that are critical for food security. By conserving blue carbon ecosystems—such as mangroves, salt marshes, and seagrasses—they play an important role in climate change mitigation and adaptation. And by preserving iconic landscapes and wildlife, they support sustainable tourism and cultural heritage.

The challenge, however, is ensuring that MPAs and the Blue Economy are not treated as separate agendas but as interconnected strategies. The Blue Economy cannot thrive if its ecological foundation is degraded, while MPAs cannot succeed in isolation from broader economic and social systems. Achieving this balance requires strong governance frameworks, innovative financing mechanisms, the deployment of advanced technologies, and inclusive stakeholder engagement. It also requires clear alignment with global goals, such as the United Nations Sustainable Development Goals, particularly Goal 14 on Life Below Water.

This book explores the critical relationship between the Blue Economy and MPAs, analyzing how the two can work in synergy to deliver ecological resilience, sustainable livelihoods, and long-term economic benefits. It examines the principles underpinning the Blue Economy, the ecological significance of MPAs, the governance and policy frameworks that support them, and the economic and social opportunities they create. It also considers the role of innovation, climate resilience, and accountability in ensuring that both strategies deliver on their promises.

By taking a principle-based, globally relevant approach, this book avoids narrow case studies and instead offers insights applicable across diverse regions and contexts. It is written for policymakers, researchers, practitioners, and stakeholders who seek to understand how to build a sustainable and inclusive ocean future. Ultimately, the integration of MPAs into the broader framework of the Blue Economy provides a pathway to balance conservation with economic growth, ensuring that the oceans remain vibrant, resilient, and abundant for generations to come.

Chapter 1: Foundations of the Blue Economy

The Blue Economy represents a transformative vision for harnessing the ocean's resources in ways that promote economic growth, social inclusion, and environmental sustainability. Rooted in the idea that healthy ecosystems underpin long-term prosperity, it shifts the paradigm from exploitation to stewardship. This chapter lays the groundwork by exploring the principles, objectives, and key sectors that define the Blue Economy. It examines both the opportunities and the challenges inherent in aligning economic development with marine conservation. By establishing these foundations, the chapter provides the context for understanding how MPAs contribute to sustainable ocean governance.

Understanding the Blue Economy

The Blue Economy is a holistic approach to managing the world's oceans and coastal resources that seeks to balance economic development with environmental sustainability and social inclusion. Unlike traditional models of growth that treat natural resources as unlimited, the Blue Economy emphasizes the sustainable use of marine ecosystems to ensure they remain productive and resilient. It reflects a recognition that the oceans are not only a source of food, minerals, and energy but also a critical foundation for climate regulation, cultural identity, and human well-being. At its core, the Blue Economy is about shifting away from exploitative practices toward stewardship and long-term prosperity.

The Blue Economy covers a wide range of activities, from fisheries and aquaculture to shipping, tourism, renewable energy, and biotechnology. Each of these sectors has the potential to generate wealth, but they also carry risks of overuse and degradation if not managed sustainably. For instance, fisheries can contribute to food security and employment, but unsustainable practices lead to overfishing and ecosystem collapse. Renewable marine energy sources such as offshore wind and tidal power offer opportunities for decarbonization, but they must be developed in ways that respect marine biodiversity and community interests. The Blue Economy ensures that growth in these areas is tied to environmental safeguards and equitable benefits.

Central to the concept is the acknowledgment of the oceans' ecological limits. Marine ecosystems provide vital services, such as carbon storage, nutrient cycling, and shoreline protection. Overexploitation, however, threatens these functions and undermines the economic potential of marine resources. The Blue Economy requires policies, regulations, and governance structures that align human activities with ecological thresholds. This means integrating environmental and social costs into economic planning, fostering innovation that reduces ecological footprints, and promoting transparency and accountability in resource management.

The Blue Economy is also closely linked with global development priorities. It aligns with the United Nations Sustainable Development Goals, particularly SDG 14 on Life Below Water, but also contributes to goals related to poverty reduction, food security, climate action, and sustainable cities. By safeguarding marine ecosystems, the Blue Economy creates opportunities for inclusive growth, especially for coastal and island communities that depend heavily on the oceans for their survival and prosperity. At the same time, it fosters resilience against climate change by protecting blue carbon ecosystems and reducing vulnerability to rising seas and extreme weather.

Ultimately, the Blue Economy is not a single policy or program but a guiding framework for reimagining the relationship between humanity and the ocean. It represents a shift in mindset: oceans are not merely spaces for extraction, but dynamic systems that must be respected, restored, and sustained. Through careful management, innovation, and cooperation, the Blue Economy provides a pathway to ensure that economic benefits do not come at the cost of ecological collapse. Instead, it envisions a future where prosperity and sustainability reinforce one another, offering a model of growth that protects the oceans while improving human well-being.

Principles and Objectives

The principles and objectives of the Blue Economy provide the foundation for aligning economic growth with the protection of marine ecosystems. At its heart lies the principle of sustainability, which demands that the use of ocean resources does not compromise their availability for future generations. This principle requires governments, industries, and communities to act responsibly, ensuring that economic activities such as fishing, tourism, energy production, and shipping remain within ecological limits. Sustainability in the Blue Economy is not only about conservation but also about securing long-term prosperity and resilience.

Another guiding principle is inclusivity. The Blue Economy recognizes that ocean resources are shared assets that must benefit all, particularly vulnerable coastal and island communities whose livelihoods depend on marine ecosystems. Inclusivity involves equitable access to resources, fair distribution of economic gains, and the participation of local stakeholders in decision-making. By ensuring inclusivity, the Blue Economy fosters social justice and enhances community ownership, creating a stronger foundation for sustainable management.

The principle of innovation is also central. Emerging technologies in monitoring, energy, aquaculture, and shipping create new opportunities to reduce environmental footprints and improve efficiency. Innovation supports better governance through real-time data collection, advances in renewable energy that reduce carbon emissions, and sustainable aquaculture practices that minimize ecological harm. Within the Blue Economy, innovation is not pursued for growth alone but as a tool for addressing sustainability challenges and expanding opportunities for responsible development.

Transparency and accountability further define the Blue Economy's framework. Marine resources are often vulnerable to mismanagement, illegal activities, and corruption. Establishing transparent governance systems ensures that decisions are evidence-based, inclusive, and aligned with long-term ecological goals. Accountability, in turn, demands effective enforcement, monitoring, and reporting mechanisms so that activities within the Blue Economy are consistent with agreed standards. This principle builds trust among stakeholders and enhances compliance with regulations.

The objectives of the Blue Economy translate these principles into actionable goals. One objective is the conservation of biodiversity and ecosystem services. Healthy marine systems underpin food security, coastal protection, and climate regulation, making their preservation essential for both ecological and economic reasons. Another objective is the promotion of sustainable livelihoods and economic diversification. By supporting industries such as renewable energy, sustainable aquaculture, and eco-tourism, the Blue Economy reduces dependence on extractive practices and opens new avenues for inclusive growth.

A further objective is climate resilience. Oceans absorb heat and carbon dioxide, making them central to climate regulation, yet they are increasingly stressed by rising temperatures, acidification, and sea level rise. Protecting blue carbon ecosystems and integrating climate adaptation into marine management are vital goals. Finally, the Blue Economy seeks to foster global cooperation. The interconnectedness of marine systems requires collective responsibility, and objectives such as achieving international biodiversity targets and enhancing marine spatial planning rely on collaboration across borders.

Together, these principles and objectives establish the foundation for a Blue Economy that balances ecological integrity, economic opportunity, and social equity. They provide a roadmap for managing marine resources in a way that sustains life, supports prosperity, and ensures resilience in the face of growing global challenges.

Key Sectors and Activities

The Blue Economy encompasses a wide range of sectors and activities that utilize ocean and coastal resources while aiming to ensure their long-term sustainability. These sectors are diverse, spanning traditional industries such as fisheries and shipping as well as emerging areas like renewable marine energy and biotechnology. Each sector contributes in different ways to livelihoods, food security, energy supply, and economic opportunity, while also carrying risks if mismanaged.

Fisheries and aquaculture remain at the core of the Blue Economy. Fisheries supply protein for billions of people, particularly in developing nations, and provide jobs for coastal communities. However, overfishing and destructive practices have strained marine ecosystems. The Blue Economy promotes sustainable fisheries management by setting catch limits, reducing bycatch, and restoring habitats. Aquaculture, when conducted sustainably, can help meet growing demand for seafood without depleting wild stocks, though it requires careful regulation to prevent pollution, disease, and habitat loss.

Shipping and maritime transport are another cornerstone of the Blue Economy, facilitating global trade and connecting economies. As one of the largest commercial uses of the oceans, shipping contributes significantly to economic growth but also generates emissions, waste, and risks of oil spills. Integrating sustainability into this sector involves adopting cleaner fuels, improving vessel efficiency, and establishing international regulations to minimize environmental impacts. A sustainable maritime transport system is essential for balancing global commerce with ocean health.

Marine tourism also plays a significant role, offering opportunities for recreation, cultural exchange, and economic development. From coastal resorts to ecotourism ventures, tourism creates income for local communities and strengthens appreciation for marine biodiversity. Yet, if unmanaged, it can lead to overcrowding, pollution, and habitat destruction. The Blue Economy promotes responsible tourism practices that preserve natural and cultural heritage, ensuring that tourism benefits both people and ecosystems.

Renewable marine energy is an expanding sector within the Blue Economy. Offshore wind farms, tidal power, and wave energy projects hold immense potential to contribute to the global transition away from fossil fuels. These technologies harness the power of the sea to provide clean energy while reducing greenhouse gas emissions. Their development, however, must consider potential impacts on marine life and coastal communities, requiring careful planning and monitoring to ensure ecological compatibility.

Marine biotechnology represents a frontier of innovation in the Blue Economy. It involves using marine organisms for pharmaceuticals, cosmetics, industrial applications, and food products. The oceans hold immense genetic diversity with potential for breakthroughs in medicine and sustainable materials. At the same time, access to genetic resources raises issues of ownership, benefit-sharing, and conservation, highlighting the need for ethical frameworks in this rapidly evolving sector.

Coastal protection and restoration activities are also becoming essential components of the Blue Economy. These include restoring mangroves, coral reefs, and seagrass beds that protect shorelines, store carbon, and provide habitats for marine life. Such efforts not only safeguard ecosystems but also create jobs in restoration industries and reduce vulnerabilities to climate change.

Each of these sectors illustrates the scope of the Blue Economy, showing both opportunities for sustainable growth and the risks of mismanagement. By embedding sustainability into every activity, the Blue Economy ensures that marine resources remain productive and resilient, supporting human well-being and planetary health.

Challenges to Sustainable Ocean Use

The sustainable use of ocean resources is increasingly constrained by a complex set of environmental, social, and economic challenges. These challenges arise from both direct human activities and broader systemic pressures, such as climate change and globalization.

Addressing them is essential for ensuring that the oceans continue to provide food, energy, livelihoods, and ecological services without being degraded beyond recovery.

One of the most pressing challenges is overfishing. Demand for seafood has risen sharply, and many fisheries are being exploited at or beyond their biological limits. Unsustainable fishing practices not only reduce fish populations but also harm habitats and disrupt marine food webs. Illegal, unreported, and unregulated fishing further undermines conservation efforts, depriving coastal communities of income and weakening governance. Overfishing threatens the long-term viability of fisheries and food security, making sustainable management an urgent priority.

Pollution represents another major obstacle to sustainable ocean use. Land-based sources such as agricultural runoff, untreated sewage, and plastic waste account for a significant portion of marine pollution. Oil spills, ship discharges, and chemical contaminants add to the burden. Pollution degrades water quality, damages ecosystems, and poses risks to human health through contaminated seafood and recreational waters. Plastic pollution in particular has become a global concern, with microplastics infiltrating marine food chains and even entering human consumption. Controlling pollution requires coordinated strategies across sectors and national boundaries.

Climate change intensifies these pressures by altering the physical and chemical conditions of the oceans. Rising sea temperatures, ocean acidification, and sea-level rise affect ecosystems, fisheries, and coastal infrastructure. Coral reefs are bleaching, species are shifting their ranges, and storms are becoming more destructive. Climate change not only undermines biodiversity but also increases risks for communities dependent on marine and coastal resources. Efforts to build resilience into ocean management must account for these accelerating impacts.

Habitat loss and degradation further weaken the capacity of oceans to sustain life. Coastal development, dredging, destructive fishing, and industrial activities contribute to the destruction of mangroves, seagrasses, coral reefs, and wetlands. These ecosystems are vital for biodiversity, shoreline protection, and carbon storage. Their loss reduces the oceans' resilience and undermines the ecological services on which both people and economies depend. Protecting and restoring habitats is therefore central to sustainable ocean use.

Governance challenges compound these environmental issues. The oceans are shared resources, yet their management is fragmented across multiple jurisdictions, institutions, and legal frameworks. Conflicting interests between conservation, industry, and local communities often lead to weak enforcement of regulations. In international waters, governance is even more difficult due to the absence of a single authority. Without effective coordination, policies risk being inconsistent or ineffective, leaving ecosystems vulnerable to exploitation.

Economic pressures also play a role. Coastal and island nations often rely heavily on ocean-based industries for income and employment. Balancing the short-term benefits of resource exploitation with the long-term need for sustainability is difficult, especially where poverty and limited institutional capacity exist. The drive for immediate economic returns can overshadow the necessity of conservation and stewardship.

Sustainable ocean use requires addressing these interlinked challenges through stronger governance, innovative solutions, and international cooperation. Only by tackling overfishing, pollution, climate impacts, habitat loss, and governance weaknesses can the full potential of the oceans be realized in ways that benefit both people and the planet.

Role of MPAs Within the Blue Economy

MPAs are a cornerstone of sustainable ocean management and play an essential role within the framework of the Blue Economy. By designating specific areas of the ocean for conservation and regulated use, MPAs safeguard marine ecosystems, preserve biodiversity, and support long-term economic and social benefits. They provide the ecological foundation upon which sustainable development of marine resources depends, making them integral to aligning economic activity with environmental protection.

One of the primary roles of MPAs in the Blue Economy is the protection of biodiversity. Healthy ecosystems underpin many of the goods and services that contribute to human well-being and economic prosperity. MPAs create safe havens where ecosystems can regenerate, fish populations can recover, and habitats can remain intact. This not only ensures the survival of marine species but also stabilizes ecological functions that sustain fisheries, tourism, and climate regulation. In this way, MPAs directly reinforce the principle of sustainability that lies at the heart of the Blue Economy.

MPAs also contribute to food security and livelihoods by sustaining fish stocks. By protecting spawning grounds and nursery habitats, MPAs allow fish populations to replenish, which in turn benefits adjacent fishing areas through a spillover effect. This helps maintain the productivity of fisheries while ensuring that fishing communities have access to resources in the long term. By embedding MPAs into the broader fisheries management framework, the Blue Economy ensures that conservation and food production complement rather than compete with each other.

Climate change mitigation and adaptation represent another critical function of MPAs. Coastal and marine ecosystems such as mangroves, seagrasses, and salt marshes are important carbon sinks, often referred to as blue carbon ecosystems. By protecting these habitats within MPAs, carbon sequestration is enhanced, contributing to global climate goals. Additionally, MPAs strengthen resilience against climate impacts by maintaining ecosystems that protect shorelines from erosion, buffer storm surges, and reduce the vulnerability of coastal communities. This dual role in mitigation and adaptation demonstrates how MPAs are vital tools in climate-responsive Blue Economy strategies.

From an economic perspective, MPAs generate opportunities in marine tourism and recreation. Well-managed MPAs attract visitors who seek experiences of pristine natural environments, supporting local businesses and creating jobs. Sustainable tourism within MPAs adds value to conservation efforts by linking ecological integrity with long-term revenue generation. This integration of ecological protection and economic activity exemplifies how MPAs operate as key assets within the Blue Economy.

MPAs also enhance governance by promoting integrated and participatory management. Their establishment often involves collaboration among governments, communities, industries, and civil society, fostering inclusive decision-making and accountability. This strengthens the social foundations of the Blue Economy by ensuring that stakeholders share responsibility for the sustainable use of resources.

The role of MPAs within the Blue Economy is to provide stability, resilience, and sustainability across ecological, social, and economic dimensions. They act as anchors for conservation while enabling responsible economic activity, ensuring that marine resources remain productive and valuable for future generations.

Chapter 2: Ecological Significance of Marine Protected Areas

MPAs are vital instruments for conserving ocean biodiversity and maintaining ecosystem functions that sustain human life. By safeguarding habitats, species, and ecological processes, MPAs strengthen the resilience of marine environments in the face of mounting pressures such as overfishing, habitat loss, and climate change. This chapter explores the ecological significance of MPAs, highlighting their roles in biodiversity conservation, habitat protection, carbon storage, and the creation of interconnected ecological networks. Understanding these contributions is essential for appreciating how MPAs underpin both environmental health and the long-term goals of the Blue Economy.

Defining MPAs and Their Categories

MPAs are clearly defined geographical spaces in the ocean that are managed to achieve the long-term conservation of biodiversity, ecosystems, and associated cultural and economic values. They are established through legal or policy frameworks that regulate human activity to varying degrees, with the aim of protecting marine environments from overexploitation and degradation. MPAs are central to efforts to safeguard the ecological integrity of the oceans while maintaining their ability to provide food, jobs, climate regulation, and cultural benefits. Their definitions vary across countries and institutions, but the unifying element is that they are formally designated areas where human activities are restricted or guided in order to conserve marine resources.

The International Union for Conservation of Nature (IUCN) provides one of the most widely recognized definitions of MPAs. According to the IUCN, an MPA is "a clearly defined geographical space, recognized, dedicated, and managed through legal or other effective means, to achieve the long-term conservation of nature with associated ecosystem services and cultural values." This definition emphasizes both the conservation objectives and the socio-economic and cultural dimensions of marine management. MPAs are not designed to exclude human activity entirely; instead, they balance conservation goals with sustainable use, ensuring that ecosystems can continue to function while supporting human well-being.

MPAs can be categorized into different types based on the level of protection and the specific objectives they serve. The most stringent are no-take zones, where extractive activities such as fishing, mining, and drilling are prohibited. These areas are critical for allowing ecosystems to regenerate and for protecting vulnerable species and habitats. No-take zones often serve as ecological benchmarks, providing scientists with undisturbed reference areas to study natural processes and assess the impacts of human activity elsewhere.

Another category is multiple-use MPAs, where activities such as fishing, tourism, and aquaculture may be allowed but are regulated to prevent ecological harm. These MPAs often include zoning arrangements that allocate different areas for specific uses, ensuring that conservation and sustainable economic activity can coexist. For example, one zone may be reserved for low-impact tourism, another for artisanal fishing, and another for strict biodiversity protection. This flexible approach recognizes that conservation outcomes can be achieved while still supporting livelihoods and economic development.

Seasonal or temporary MPAs are also used in some contexts. These are areas that restrict human activity during specific times of the year to protect spawning fish, migrating species, or breeding grounds. By tailoring protections to biological cycles, seasonal MPAs provide targeted conservation benefits while minimizing disruption to economic activities at other times.

In addition, there are large-scale MPAs, sometimes referred to as marine reserves or sanctuaries, that encompass vast areas of ocean and protect entire ecosystems. These areas are particularly important for highly migratory species, wide-ranging ecological processes, and the protection of relatively pristine marine environments. Large-scale MPAs also contribute significantly to global targets for ocean protection, such as the goal of protecting 30 percent of the world's oceans by 2030.

Defining MPAs and their categories highlights the diversity of approaches available for marine conservation. While some emphasize strict protection, others seek to balance ecological preservation with human use. This flexibility makes MPAs adaptable to different ecological contexts, governance systems, and socio-economic needs, strengthening their role as key instruments in sustainable ocean management and the Blue Economy.

Biodiversity Conservation and Habitat Protection

Biodiversity conservation and habitat protection are central objectives of MPAs and essential components of sustainable ocean management. Oceans host an extraordinary variety of life, ranging from microscopic plankton to the largest mammals on Earth, and this biodiversity underpins ecological stability, food security, and human well-being. However, human activities such as overfishing, pollution, and coastal development have placed unprecedented pressure on marine ecosystems. MPAs provide a framework to safeguard biodiversity and maintain the ecological processes that support both nature and people.

One of the key contributions of MPAs to biodiversity conservation is the preservation of species richness and abundance. By reducing or eliminating destructive activities within designated areas, MPAs create safe zones where marine life can recover and thrive. Fish populations, in particular, benefit from protection as MPAs allow individuals to grow larger and reproduce more successfully. This replenishment effect enhances population resilience and contributes to the recovery of species that have been overexploited. In addition to fish, MPAs also protect vulnerable and endangered species such as sea turtles, sharks, marine mammals, and seabirds, which are often threatened by human pressures in unprotected waters.

Habitat protection is another vital function of MPAs. Marine habitats such as coral reefs, mangroves, seagrass beds, kelp forests, and salt marshes provide the physical and biological foundation for countless species. These habitats serve as nurseries, feeding grounds, and shelter, supporting complex food webs and maintaining ecosystem balance. By safeguarding these areas from damaging activities like trawling, dredging, or unregulated coastal development, MPAs preserve the structures and processes that sustain marine biodiversity. Healthy habitats are not only critical for wildlife but also provide services that benefit humans, such as coastal protection, carbon storage, and water purification.

MPAs also play a role in maintaining genetic diversity within marine populations. Genetic diversity is essential for species' ability to adapt to changing environmental conditions, including those driven by climate change. By protecting large, interconnected habitats and reducing stressors, MPAs support the maintenance of viable breeding populations and help prevent genetic erosion. This ensures that species retain the capacity to evolve and remain resilient in the face of future challenges.

In addition, MPAs help restore ecological integrity by re-establishing natural interactions between species and ecosystems. For example, by protecting predator populations, MPAs can restore balance to food webs and prevent trophic cascades that occur when key species are removed. Restored ecological dynamics improve the overall health and stability of marine ecosystems, increasing their ability to provide services that humans rely upon.

Biodiversity conservation within MPAs also contributes to broader global goals, such as the Convention on Biological Diversity and the United Nations Sustainable Development Goals. Protecting biodiversity through MPAs is not only about safeguarding wildlife but also about securing the ecological foundation of sustainable development. By conserving biodiversity and protecting habitats, MPAs ensure that ecosystems continue to function effectively, support economic activities, and build resilience to environmental change.

Through these mechanisms, MPAs serve as vital tools for conserving the richness of life in the oceans and for maintaining the health of habitats that sustain both ecological and human systems. They are a critical investment in the long-term stability and productivity of marine environments.

Ecosystem Services and Blue Carbon

Marine ecosystems provide a wide array of services that are fundamental to human well-being, economic prosperity, and planetary stability. These benefits, known as ecosystem services, encompass provisioning services such as food and raw materials, regulating services such as climate regulation and coastal protection, cultural services such as recreation and heritage, and supporting services such as nutrient cycling and habitat provision. MPAs safeguard these services by protecting the ecological integrity of ecosystems, ensuring that they continue to function and provide value to present and future generations.

One of the most visible ecosystem services is food provision. Fisheries supply a significant portion of the world's protein, and healthy marine ecosystems ensure the replenishment of fish stocks. By protecting spawning grounds, nursery habitats, and feeding areas, MPAs support the regeneration of fish populations, which benefits adjacent fishing zones through the spillover effect. This contributes not only to food security but also to livelihoods for coastal communities that rely heavily on fisheries.

Another crucial service is coastal protection. Habitats such as coral reefs, mangroves, and seagrass beds act as natural buffers against storms, waves, and erosion. Coral reefs dissipate wave energy, mangroves stabilize shorelines with their root systems, and seagrasses trap sediments, improving water clarity. The loss of these habitats leaves coastal communities vulnerable to flooding, property damage, and displacement. By safeguarding these ecosystems, MPAs reduce risks to human settlements and infrastructure, thereby lowering the costs of disaster recovery and adaptation measures.

Water quality regulation is another important service provided by marine ecosystems. Wetlands, seagrass beds, and mangroves filter pollutants, trap sediments, and recycle nutrients, maintaining the health of coastal waters. This natural purification system supports marine life and reduces the burden on human-built infrastructure. Protecting these habitats within MPAs ensures that ecosystems continue to perform these functions, which are critical for both biodiversity and human populations.

Among the regulating services, carbon sequestration—commonly referred to as blue carbon—is increasingly recognized for its role in addressing climate change. Blue carbon ecosystems, including mangroves, seagrasses, and salt marshes, capture and store significant amounts of carbon dioxide in their biomass and sediments. These ecosystems sequester carbon at rates far higher than many terrestrial forests, making them powerful natural allies in climate mitigation. When degraded, however, they release stored carbon back into the atmosphere, contributing to greenhouse gas emissions. Protecting and restoring blue carbon habitats through MPAs enhances their capacity to act as carbon sinks, directly supporting global climate targets.

Cultural and recreational services also benefit from healthy marine ecosystems. MPAs often preserve areas of scenic beauty, cultural heritage, and spiritual significance. They provide opportunities for recreation, education, and ecotourism, which generate economic benefits and foster public appreciation for marine conservation. These cultural dimensions strengthen the connection between people and the sea, building support for sustainable ocean management.

By securing ecosystem services and protecting blue carbon habitats, MPAs contribute to both ecological resilience and human prosperity. They ensure that marine ecosystems continue to sustain fisheries, regulate climate, protect coasts, and provide cultural and recreational value. These contributions demonstrate how MPAs are not only conservation tools but also essential pillars of the Blue Economy, linking ecological integrity with sustainable economic growth.

Resilience to Climate Change

MPAs play a critical role in enhancing the resilience of ecosystems and human communities to the impacts of climate change. As oceans warm, acidify, and experience rising sea levels, marine ecosystems face unprecedented stress. Coral reefs are bleaching, fish are shifting their ranges, and coastal communities are increasingly vulnerable to flooding and erosion. MPAs, by safeguarding biodiversity and habitats, create conditions that allow ecosystems to adapt more effectively to these changes while continuing to provide vital services for human well-being.

One of the primary ways MPAs strengthen resilience is by reducing cumulative pressures on ecosystems. Many marine environments are already affected by pollution, overfishing, and habitat destruction. These pressures weaken ecosystems, making them less able to withstand climate-related disturbances such as heatwaves or storms. By regulating or restricting harmful activities, MPAs provide ecosystems with space to recover and maintain ecological integrity. This healthier baseline enables marine species and habitats to better absorb and adapt to the shocks of climate variability and long-term change.

MPAs also support climate resilience by conserving biodiversity. Ecosystems with higher biodiversity tend to be more resilient because they include a greater diversity of species that can fulfill essential ecological functions even if some species decline. For example, protecting a variety of herbivorous fish helps maintain coral reef health by controlling algae growth, which in turn supports reef recovery after bleaching events. Biodiverse ecosystems are more adaptable to changing conditions, ensuring the continued delivery of services such as food provision and shoreline protection.

Protecting blue carbon ecosystems within MPAs is another significant contribution to climate resilience. Mangroves, seagrasses, and salt marshes not only store vast amounts of carbon but also buffer coasts against sea-level rise and storm surges. Their root systems stabilize sediments, reduce erosion, and provide natural defenses that are often more cost-effective than artificial infrastructure. By conserving these habitats, MPAs help shield coastal communities from climate-related hazards while enhancing global efforts to mitigate greenhouse gas emissions.

MPAs further contribute to resilience by providing safe havens for species under climate stress. As ocean temperatures rise, many marine organisms are forced to migrate in search of suitable conditions. MPAs that are strategically located along migratory routes or that protect a range of habitats can serve as refuges, enabling species to survive and adjust to shifting environments. Networks of MPAs that are ecologically connected can facilitate the movement of species and genetic exchange, strengthening adaptability across broader regions.

For human communities, the resilience benefits of MPAs are equally significant. By sustaining fisheries, protecting coastal infrastructure through habitat conservation, and supporting tourism and cultural values, MPAs reduce vulnerability to climate-driven disruptions. They also provide a platform for inclusive governance and community engagement, ensuring that local knowledge and priorities are incorporated into adaptation strategies.

Through these mechanisms, MPAs contribute to both ecological and social resilience in the face of climate change. They provide ecosystems and communities with the capacity to withstand shocks, recover from disturbances, and adapt to long-term changes. As climate impacts intensify, the role of MPAs in fostering resilience becomes increasingly central to sustainable ocean governance and the broader objectives of the Blue Economy.

Connectivity and Ecological Networks

Connectivity and ecological networks are fundamental concepts in marine conservation and are critical to the effectiveness of MPAs. Oceans are highly dynamic systems where species, nutrients, and energy move continuously across large spatial scales. Fish migrate between feeding and spawning grounds, larvae drift with ocean currents, and predators travel vast distances in search of food. To conserve biodiversity and maintain ecosystem functions, it is not enough to protect isolated patches of habitat. MPAs must be designed and managed as part of interconnected ecological networks that reflect the natural linkages within marine systems.

Ecological connectivity refers to the movement and exchange of organisms, genetic material, and ecological processes across habitats and regions. For many marine species, life cycles depend on different habitats at different stages. Coral reefs, mangroves, and seagrass beds, for example, are interconnected ecosystems that support one another. Juvenile fish may grow in mangroves or seagrasses before moving to coral reefs as adults, while nutrient flows between these ecosystems sustain productivity. Protecting only one habitat type in isolation risks undermining the broader ecological network. By ensuring connectivity among ecosystems, MPAs preserve these vital linkages that maintain resilience and productivity.

Networks of MPAs expand this concept by protecting multiple sites that together safeguard species and habitats across their ranges. Instead of functioning as isolated conservation areas, MPAs can be strategically linked to form a coherent system that delivers broader ecological benefits. Networks provide redundancy, meaning that if one site is damaged by a disturbance such as a storm or bleaching event, others can compensate by supporting species recovery and recolonization. Well-designed networks ensure that critical habitats such as spawning grounds, migratory corridors, and nursery areas are all represented and protected.

Connectivity is also essential for maintaining genetic diversity, which strengthens the adaptive capacity of species to respond to environmental changes. Populations that are connected through larval dispersal and migration have greater opportunities for genetic exchange, reducing the risks of inbreeding and local extinction. By protecting areas that facilitate these exchanges, MPAs contribute to the long-term evolutionary potential of marine species. This is particularly important under climate change, as species with higher genetic diversity are better able to adapt to shifting conditions.

From a governance perspective, ecological networks of MPAs often extend across political boundaries, requiring cooperation between countries and jurisdictions. Migratory species such as tuna, whales, and turtles move across vast oceanic regions, making regional and international coordination essential. Multinational MPA networks, such as those established through regional seas conventions, provide frameworks for collaboration, data sharing, and joint management. These efforts strengthen global commitments to biodiversity conservation while recognizing the transboundary nature of marine ecosystems.

In addition to ecological benefits, connectivity and networks also enhance the resilience of human communities. By sustaining fisheries through spillover effects, protecting coastlines across multiple regions, and supporting ecotourism opportunities, interconnected MPAs provide broader social and economic value than isolated sites.

Connectivity and ecological networks therefore represent a strategic approach to marine conservation. They ensure that MPAs function not as isolated islands of protection but as components of a larger, resilient system. By recognizing the natural linkages within marine environments and designing MPAs to reflect them, conservation efforts can secure biodiversity, sustain ecosystem services, and strengthen the foundations of the Blue Economy.

Chapter 3: Governance and Policy Frameworks

Effective governance and policy frameworks form the backbone of MPA management and their integration within the Blue Economy. Strong legal, institutional, and regulatory systems ensure that MPAs are more than symbolic designations, providing the mechanisms necessary for enforcement, accountability, and long-term success. This chapter examines the role of international agreements, national legislation, institutional arrangements, and marine spatial planning in shaping conservation outcomes. It also highlights the importance of stakeholder engagement and co-management approaches, showing how inclusive governance fosters legitimacy, compliance, and resilience in marine conservation efforts.

International Conventions and Agreements

International conventions and agreements form the backbone of global efforts to conserve the oceans and regulate human activities within them. Because marine ecosystems cross national boundaries and extend into areas beyond national jurisdiction, cooperation among states is essential for effective governance. MPAs, as a key tool for biodiversity conservation and sustainable ocean management, are strongly influenced by international legal frameworks that set standards, provide guidance, and establish obligations for states. These agreements create consistency, promote accountability, and facilitate collaboration in achieving shared goals for the Blue Economy and marine conservation.

One of the most significant frameworks is the United Nations Convention on the Law of the Sea (UNCLOS). Adopted in 1982, UNCLOS is often described as the "constitution for the oceans." It defines maritime zones, including territorial seas, exclusive economic zones, and the high seas, and sets out states' rights and responsibilities. For MPAs, UNCLOS provides the legal foundation for establishing protected areas within national jurisdictions and highlights the duty of states to protect and preserve the marine environment. Although it does not specify exact mechanisms for MPAs, it obliges states to prevent, reduce, and control pollution and overexploitation, which indirectly supports conservation efforts.

The Convention on Biological Diversity (CBD) is another critical instrument. Adopted in 1992, the CBD commits parties to conserve biodiversity, ensure sustainable use of natural resources, and promote equitable sharing of benefits. The CBD's Aichi Biodiversity Targets included the well-known commitment to protect at least 10 percent of coastal and marine areas by 2020. Building on this, the Kunming-Montreal Global Biodiversity Framework set a more ambitious target of protecting 30 percent of the world's land and ocean by 2030. These commitments have driven the expansion of MPAs worldwide and continue to shape national policies and strategies.

The Convention on International Trade in Endangered Species of Wild Fauna and Flora (CITES) also contributes to marine conservation by regulating international trade in endangered marine species, such as certain sharks, corals, and sea turtles. By controlling trade and ensuring it is sustainable, CITES complements MPA efforts by addressing pressures that extend beyond protected boundaries. Similarly, the Convention on Migratory Species (CMS) provides a framework for conserving species that move across national borders, ensuring that migratory routes and habitats are protected through international cooperation.

The International Maritime Organization (IMO) plays a role in designating Particularly Sensitive Sea Areas (PSSAs), which restrict shipping activities to protect ecologically important or vulnerable areas. These designations often overlap with MPAs and enhance their effectiveness by controlling maritime impacts such as pollution, noise, and collisions with marine life. The IMO also enforces regulations to reduce emissions and manage ballast water, indirectly supporting marine ecosystem health.

Regional agreements further strengthen international cooperation. Instruments such as the Barcelona Convention for the Mediterranean and the OSPAR Convention for the North-East Atlantic establish frameworks for regional MPA networks, promoting collaboration among neighboring states. These agreements often address shared challenges such as pollution, fisheries management, and habitat protection, tailoring solutions to regional contexts.

International conventions and agreements provide the legal and political architecture necessary to achieve large-scale marine protection. By setting targets, guiding national implementation, and fostering collaboration across jurisdictions, they enable the establishment and effective management of MPAs as part of a global strategy for biodiversity conservation and the Blue Economy. Without these collective commitments, efforts to safeguard the oceans would remain fragmented and far less effective.

National Legislation and Regulations

National legislation and regulations are the primary mechanisms through which countries establish, manage, and enforce MPAs. While international conventions provide the overarching framework for marine conservation, it is at the national level that commitments are translated into concrete policies and actions. Effective laws and regulatory systems ensure that MPAs are not only designated but also implemented and managed in ways that balance ecological integrity with economic and social needs. National frameworks thus form the operational backbone of sustainable ocean governance and are central to integrating MPAs into the Blue Economy.

One of the main functions of national legislation is to provide the legal authority to create MPAs. Many countries have enacted specific marine conservation laws or broader environmental acts that empower governments to designate marine areas as protected. These laws define the objectives of MPAs, such as conserving biodiversity, sustaining fisheries, or protecting cultural heritage, and establish the processes for delineating boundaries and setting restrictions. By codifying these powers in law, governments provide clarity and legitimacy, ensuring that MPAs are recognized and enforceable.

Regulations derived from these laws outline the specific rules governing activities within MPAs. Depending on the category and objectives of the protected area, regulations may prohibit certain activities such as trawling, mining, or drilling, while allowing others like small-scale fishing or ecotourism under strict guidelines. Zoning systems are often employed to allocate different uses to different parts of an MPA, ensuring that conservation goals are met while allowing sustainable economic activities. Regulations also typically establish penalties for violations, reinforcing compliance and accountability.

National legislation also plays a role in integrating MPAs into broader marine and coastal management frameworks. In many countries, MPAs are part of marine spatial planning systems, which coordinate different uses of marine space to reduce conflicts and enhance sustainability. Laws may require MPAs to be considered alongside fisheries management, shipping, energy development, and tourism, ensuring that conservation objectives are mainstreamed into national ocean policy. This integrated approach is essential for aligning MPAs with the principles of the Blue Economy.

Enforcement mechanisms are another critical component of national regulations. Effective management requires the capacity to monitor activities, detect violations, and impose penalties. Some countries rely on traditional enforcement tools such as patrols by coast guards or marine rangers, while others employ technological solutions such as satellite monitoring, drones, and vessel-tracking systems. Strong enforcement ensures that MPAs achieve their intended conservation outcomes and provides credibility to the broader governance framework.

Public participation and community involvement are often incorporated into national legislation, reflecting the importance of inclusivity in marine conservation. Laws may mandate stakeholder consultations before establishing MPAs or provide for co-management arrangements that involve local communities in decision-making and enforcement. Such provisions help build local support, enhance compliance, and ensure that MPAs contribute to social as well as ecological objectives.

Finally, national legislation and regulations create the foundation for aligning domestic policies with international commitments. By enacting laws that incorporate global targets such as the goal of protecting 30 percent of the ocean by 2030, governments demonstrate accountability and contribute to collective progress. In this way, national frameworks act as the critical link between global ambition and local action.

Through these legal and regulatory structures, countries provide the authority, rules, and enforcement necessary to establish and maintain effective MPAs. Strong national legislation ensures that marine conservation is not an aspirational goal but a practical, enforceable reality that contributes directly to the Blue Economy and long-term sustainability.

Institutional Arrangements

Institutional arrangements are the organizational structures, roles, and relationships that determine how MPAs are established, managed, and monitored. Effective arrangements are essential to ensure that MPAs fulfill their conservation objectives while contributing to the broader goals of the Blue Economy. These structures involve multiple actors, ranging from government agencies and local authorities to non-governmental organizations, research institutions, and community groups. By clarifying responsibilities, coordinating actions, and fostering collaboration, institutional arrangements provide the governance framework necessary for sustainable marine management.

At the national level, central government agencies typically hold the authority to designate MPAs and oversee their management.

Ministries of environment, fisheries, or maritime affairs often take the lead in drafting policies, developing regulations, and ensuring compliance. In some cases, responsibilities are shared across ministries, with one agency focusing on biodiversity conservation and another on resource management or enforcement. Clearly defined mandates are critical to avoid overlaps, gaps, or conflicts in governance. Where coordination is weak, MPAs may suffer from inconsistent enforcement or fragmented decision-making.

Decentralized governance is also common in many countries, particularly where coastal communities are closely tied to marine resources. Local governments may be given the authority to manage MPAs within their jurisdictions, often under national legal frameworks. This approach can increase efficiency and responsiveness, as local authorities are often better positioned to address site-specific challenges. Decentralization also enhances community engagement by bringing decision-making closer to those most affected. However, it requires adequate capacity, resources, and oversight to ensure that local management aligns with national and international commitments.

Non-governmental organizations (NGOs) play an important role in institutional arrangements for MPAs. Many NGOs contribute technical expertise, funding, and advocacy that support both the establishment and operation of MPAs. They may also act as intermediaries between governments and local communities, helping to build trust and encourage participation. In some contexts, NGOs are directly involved in co-management agreements, sharing responsibilities with government agencies. This collaborative model can strengthen conservation outcomes by combining scientific knowledge, financial resources, and community support.

Research institutions and universities also contribute to institutional arrangements by providing the scientific basis for decision-making. Through ecological monitoring, data analysis, and policy research, they inform management strategies and help evaluate the effectiveness of MPAs. Scientific input ensures that conservation measures are grounded in evidence and can adapt to changing ecological and social conditions. Partnerships between researchers and managers are particularly important for fostering adaptive management, where strategies are adjusted over time based on observed outcomes.

Community-based organizations and traditional institutions often play crucial roles in ensuring that MPAs reflect local needs and knowledge. In many regions, customary marine tenure systems and traditional practices have long regulated resource use. Incorporating these systems into formal MPA governance not only enhances legitimacy but also builds on generations of local expertise. Community involvement in monitoring, enforcement, and decision-making strengthens compliance and ensures that MPAs provide tangible benefits to those who depend on them most.

Finally, institutional arrangements often extend beyond national borders. Regional organizations and international partnerships help coordinate networks of MPAs, share best practices, and harmonize management across jurisdictions. Such collaboration is particularly important for protecting migratory species and ecosystems that span multiple countries.

Institutional arrangements are thus the backbone of MPA governance. By defining roles, fostering collaboration, and integrating diverse actors, they ensure that MPAs are not isolated efforts but part of a coordinated system that supports conservation, sustainable development, and the long-term vision of the Blue Economy.

Marine Spatial Planning and Integration with MPAs

Marine Spatial Planning (MSP) is a strategic process that organizes the use of marine space to balance ecological, economic, and social objectives. It provides a framework for managing competing demands on the ocean, ensuring that activities such as fishing, shipping, tourism, energy production, and conservation can coexist in a sustainable way. Within this framework, MPAs are integrated as essential components that safeguard biodiversity, sustain ecosystem services, and support the long-term vision of the Blue Economy.

The oceans are increasingly crowded as multiple sectors expand their activities. Without careful planning, conflicts can arise between conservation efforts and economic uses, such as fishing versus tourism or renewable energy development versus shipping routes. MSP addresses these conflicts by identifying priority areas for different uses, setting spatial and temporal boundaries, and creating rules that minimize negative impacts. By embedding MPAs into the broader spatial plan, conservation measures are harmonized with other marine activities rather than being treated as isolated interventions.

A central feature of MSP is the ecosystem-based approach. This approach recognizes that marine ecosystems are interconnected and that human activities must be managed within ecological limits. MPAs, when integrated into MSP, serve as anchors for maintaining ecological integrity. They protect habitats critical to biodiversity, fisheries productivity, and climate resilience, ensuring that other marine uses are developed in ways that do not undermine the ecological foundation of the ocean economy. For example, MSP may designate MPAs in areas of high ecological value while steering industrial activities such as energy development to less sensitive regions.

Zoning is a key tool within MSP that supports the integration of MPAs. By dividing marine areas into zones with specific rules, planners can accommodate multiple objectives. Strictly protected MPAs may be established in ecologically sensitive areas, while multiple-use MPAs may allow sustainable fishing or tourism under regulated conditions. Surrounding zones can be designated for activities such as aquaculture or renewable energy, creating a coherent system where conservation and development complement each other. This zoning approach helps reduce conflict, increase predictability, and improve compliance.

MSP also enhances the effectiveness of MPAs by situating them within broader management strategies. For instance, MPAs that are part of an MSP network can be connected through ecological corridors, ensuring species movement and genetic exchange. MSP can also account for cumulative impacts, such as the combined effects of fishing, pollution, and climate change, and design MPA networks that maximize resilience under these pressures. By coordinating across scales, MSP ensures that MPAs are not just isolated patches of protection but integral elements of a larger, functioning ocean system.

Integration through MSP further strengthens governance by aligning the interests of multiple stakeholders. Governments, industries, communities, and conservation organizations all have a place in the planning process, ensuring that decisions reflect diverse perspectives. This participatory dimension enhances legitimacy, fosters cooperation, and builds shared responsibility for both conservation and sustainable use.

By embedding MPAs into Marine Spatial Planning, conservation and economic development can move forward together under a unified framework. MSP ensures that MPAs contribute not only to biodiversity protection but also to the sustainable and equitable management of marine resources, making them central to the success of the Blue Economy.

Stakeholder Engagement and Co-Management

Stakeholder engagement and co-management are central to the effective governance of MPAs. Because oceans support diverse interests—ranging from small-scale fishers and indigenous communities to tourism operators, conservation organizations, and national governments—successful management depends on balancing these perspectives. Engaging stakeholders ensures that MPAs are not imposed top-down but are instead developed and managed through inclusive, transparent, and participatory processes. Co-management, which involves shared responsibility between governments and local communities or other stakeholders, builds trust, enhances legitimacy, and strengthens compliance, making MPAs more resilient and effective over time.

Engagement begins with identifying the full range of stakeholders who depend on or influence marine ecosystems. These often include coastal communities whose livelihoods rely on fishing, aquaculture, or tourism, as well as industries such as shipping, energy, and biotechnology. Civil society groups, academics, and indigenous peoples bring additional perspectives, including cultural and traditional knowledge that can complement scientific expertise. Involving these groups from the outset ensures that diverse interests are represented in the design and management of MPAs, reducing conflict and fostering a sense of ownership.

Participatory processes help build consensus on the objectives, boundaries, and rules of MPAs. Public consultations, workshops, and community meetings allow stakeholders to voice concerns and contribute ideas. This inclusive dialogue enhances the legitimacy of management decisions, making it more likely that stakeholders will respect and support regulations. It also helps identify potential trade-offs between conservation and economic activities, enabling solutions that balance ecological integrity with livelihood needs. Transparency in decision-making is critical, as it prevents perceptions of exclusion and builds trust in management institutions.

Co-management arrangements go a step further by institutionalizing shared responsibility. Under this model, governments retain legal authority but delegate certain management functions to local stakeholders. Communities may take part in surveillance, enforcement, or data collection, while NGOs and research institutions may contribute technical expertise and resources. By sharing responsibilities, co-management increases efficiency and fosters collaboration between different actors. It also empowers communities, recognizing their rights and knowledge while providing them with a stake in the success of conservation efforts.

One of the advantages of stakeholder engagement and co-management is improved compliance with regulations. When communities are involved in shaping the rules, they are more likely to view them as fair and relevant. Peer monitoring and social accountability can complement formal enforcement, reducing costs and increasing effectiveness. Engagement also provides opportunities for capacity building, equipping communities with the skills and resources needed to participate actively in management. This contributes to long-term sustainability by ensuring that local institutions can carry forward conservation initiatives beyond the life of specific projects or funding cycles.

Inclusive governance also enhances equity and social justice. MPAs can impose restrictions that affect livelihoods, particularly in communities dependent on fishing or resource extraction. By involving stakeholders in management decisions, trade-offs can be addressed more fairly, and alternative livelihood opportunities can be developed. This helps mitigate negative impacts while ensuring that the benefits of conservation—such as improved fish stocks, tourism revenue, or climate resilience—are distributed equitably.

Stakeholder engagement and co-management are therefore essential for integrating social and ecological dimensions in MPA governance. They ensure that conservation is not only about protecting ecosystems but also about supporting the people who depend on them. By fostering participation, sharing responsibility, and building trust, these approaches strengthen the foundations of MPAs and contribute directly to the goals of the Blue Economy.

Chapter 4: Economic Dimensions of MPAs in the Blue Economy

MPAs are not only ecological assets but also critical drivers of economic value within the Blue Economy. By sustaining fisheries, enabling marine tourism, creating jobs, and supporting livelihoods, MPAs demonstrate how conservation and economic development can be mutually reinforcing. This chapter explores the economic dimensions of MPAs, from the valuation of ecosystem services to their role in food security and employment. It also examines the challenges of balancing conservation and development, highlighting how MPAs contribute to sustainable supply chains and long-term prosperity for coastal communities and national economies alike.

Economic Valuation of Marine Ecosystem Services

Economic valuation of marine ecosystem services is a key tool in demonstrating the tangible benefits that oceans and coasts provide to human societies. By assigning economic values to the goods and services generated by marine ecosystems, decision-makers can better appreciate their importance and justify investments in conservation, including the establishment and management of MPAs. Valuation highlights the direct and indirect contributions of marine ecosystems to the economy, helping to integrate environmental considerations into planning, budgeting, and development policies aligned with the Blue Economy.

Marine ecosystems deliver provisioning services such as fisheries, aquaculture, and raw materials. These services have clear market values because they generate products that can be sold and traded. However, the long-term sustainability of these sectors depends on the health of underlying ecosystems. By valuing the contribution of habitats like coral reefs, mangroves, and seagrass beds to fishery productivity, policymakers can recognize the cost of degradation and the benefits of protection. For example, an MPA that sustains fish stocks through habitat conservation provides measurable economic value in the form of increased catches and secure livelihoods.

Regulating services are another critical category of ecosystem benefits. These include carbon sequestration, shoreline stabilization, and water purification. Unlike provisioning services, regulating services often lack direct market prices, which can lead to their underappreciation in economic decisions. Blue carbon ecosystems—mangroves, seagrasses, and salt marshes—store vast amounts of carbon and play a vital role in climate regulation. Assigning economic values to their carbon storage capacity enables policymakers to include them in climate finance mechanisms, carbon markets, and adaptation planning. Similarly, valuing coastal protection services provided by reefs and mangroves demonstrates that investing in natural infrastructure can be more cost-effective than building artificial defenses.

Cultural services also hold significant economic value. Marine ecosystems support tourism, recreation, and cultural identity, contributing substantially to local and national economies. Pristine beaches, coral reefs, and charismatic wildlife attract millions of tourists annually, generating income for businesses and employment for communities. Valuing these services highlights the link between healthy ecosystems and economic prosperity, reinforcing the need for effective management of MPAs. In addition, cultural and spiritual values, while more difficult to quantify, can be assessed through willingness-to-pay studies or other non-market valuation methods, ensuring that these less tangible benefits are not overlooked.

Supporting services, such as nutrient cycling and habitat provision, underpin the productivity of marine ecosystems but are often invisible in traditional economic analyses. Valuation methods can estimate their contribution by linking ecological processes to economic outcomes, such as improved fishery yields or enhanced water quality. These assessments provide a more complete picture of the benefits provided by marine ecosystems, ensuring that conservation is recognized as an investment rather than a cost.

Economic valuation is also instrumental in decision-making and policy design. By comparing the economic benefits of ecosystem services with the costs of conservation or exploitation, policymakers can make informed choices about resource allocation. Valuation strengthens the case for MPAs by demonstrating their role in sustaining long-term economic benefits, reducing disaster risks, and supporting climate resilience.

Through robust valuation of ecosystem services, marine conservation becomes integrated into economic planning, making it clear that protecting biodiversity and habitats is not only an environmental necessity but also a sound economic strategy for sustaining the Blue Economy.

Sustainable Fisheries and Food Security

Sustainable fisheries are a central pillar of the Blue Economy and play a vital role in ensuring global food security. Oceans provide a significant share of the world's protein, particularly for communities in developing countries and small island states where alternative sources of food are limited. However, unsustainable fishing practices and overexploitation have placed enormous pressure on fish stocks, with many now depleted or in decline. MPAs and responsible management practices are critical to reversing these trends, securing long-term productivity, and ensuring that fisheries continue to support human well-being.

Overfishing remains one of the most urgent threats to food security. Driven by rising demand, technological advances, and weak governance in some regions, global fishing capacity has outpaced the natural regeneration of fish populations. This not only threatens biodiversity but also jeopardizes livelihoods for millions of people who depend on fishing for income and sustenance. Unsustainable practices such as bottom trawling, dynamite fishing, and bycatch of non-target species further degrade marine habitats and reduce ecosystem resilience. Sustainable fisheries management seeks to address these problems by regulating catches, protecting breeding grounds, and aligning harvesting with ecological limits.

MPAs contribute significantly to sustainable fisheries by protecting critical habitats and allowing fish populations to recover. No-take zones, where extractive activities are prohibited, act as refuges for breeding and juvenile development. Over time, these areas replenish adjacent fishing zones through spillover, where adult fish migrate beyond protected boundaries, and through the export of larvae carried by ocean currents. This replenishment enhances productivity in nearby fisheries, benefiting local communities and economies. By combining MPAs with broader fisheries management measures, such as quotas and gear restrictions, countries can achieve both conservation and food production objectives.

Food security also depends on the nutritional value provided by marine resources. Fish and seafood are rich in essential nutrients, including omega-3 fatty acids, vitamins, and minerals, making them critical to global nutrition. For many coastal populations, fish constitute the primary source of animal protein. Declines in fish stocks therefore have direct consequences for public health, particularly in vulnerable regions. Ensuring sustainable fisheries safeguards not just economic livelihoods but also the nutritional well-being of millions of people worldwide.

Aquaculture, or the farming of fish and other aquatic organisms, has grown rapidly as a response to declining wild stocks and rising demand. When practiced sustainably, aquaculture can contribute to food security by supplying affordable protein and reducing pressure on wild populations. However, it must be carefully regulated to avoid environmental impacts such as pollution, disease transmission, and habitat loss. Integrating sustainable aquaculture practices into the Blue Economy complements conservation goals while supporting growing food needs.

Effective governance is essential for achieving sustainable fisheries and food security. Transparent policies, strong enforcement, and inclusive decision-making ensure that fishing practices remain within ecological boundaries. Engagement with local communities and indigenous groups is especially important, as their traditional knowledge and stewardship practices often support sustainability.

International cooperation is also critical, as many fish stocks are migratory and cross national boundaries.

Sustainable fisheries provide a foundation for resilient food systems, supporting both global nutrition and economic stability. By aligning fisheries management with conservation through tools such as MPAs, the Blue Economy secures the long-term productivity of marine resources, ensuring that oceans can continue to feed future generations.

Marine Tourism and Recreation

Marine tourism and recreation are significant sectors within the Blue Economy, offering economic opportunities while highlighting the cultural and ecological value of the oceans. Activities such as diving, snorkeling, wildlife watching, coastal recreation, and boating attract millions of people each year, generating revenue for local economies and creating employment in hospitality, transport, and guiding services. When managed responsibly, marine tourism not only provides income but also fosters appreciation for marine ecosystems, strengthening the case for conservation and the expansion of MPAs.

Tourism linked to healthy marine ecosystems often becomes a cornerstone of local and national economies. Coral reefs, seagrass beds, mangroves, and pristine beaches are natural attractions that draw visitors seeking recreational experiences. These ecosystems provide aesthetic, cultural, and recreational services that have substantial economic value. Countries with extensive coastlines and marine biodiversity often rely heavily on tourism revenue, with MPAs serving as focal points for eco-tourism and sustainable travel. The presence of charismatic wildlife such as dolphins, whales, sea turtles, and seabirds further enhances the appeal of marine destinations.

MPAs play a vital role in sustaining marine tourism by ensuring that ecosystems remain healthy and attractive. By regulating extractive activities such as fishing and restricting damaging practices like anchoring on coral reefs, MPAs safeguard the ecological integrity that underpins tourism experiences. This protection not only enhances biodiversity but also provides tourists with opportunities to enjoy vibrant underwater landscapes and abundant marine life. The association between well-managed MPAs and high-quality tourism experiences reinforces the link between conservation and economic development.

However, marine tourism can also pose risks if it is poorly planned or unregulated. Overcrowding in popular destinations can lead to habitat degradation, pollution, and disturbances to wildlife. Uncontrolled diving or snorkeling can damage fragile coral reefs, while excessive boat traffic can cause erosion and harm sensitive species through collisions or noise. The challenge lies in ensuring that tourism is developed sustainably, with clear guidelines, limits on visitor numbers where necessary, and infrastructure designed to minimize environmental impacts. Incorporating carrying capacity assessments into tourism planning helps maintain ecological balance while ensuring positive visitor experiences.

Sustainable marine tourism practices are increasingly being promoted as part of the Blue Economy. Eco-certification programs, environmental education, and community-based tourism initiatives encourage operators and visitors to adopt low-impact practices. For example, tour operators can be required to follow codes of conduct for wildlife viewing, ensuring that encounters do not disturb or stress animals. Revenue generated from tourism can also be reinvested into MPA management, research, and local community development, creating a positive feedback loop where conservation and economic benefits reinforce one another.

Community involvement is central to successful marine tourism. Local residents often serve as guides, operators, and stewards of natural resources. Their participation ensures that tourism benefits are shared equitably and that cultural heritage is preserved alongside natural ecosystems. When communities see direct benefits from tourism, they are more likely to support conservation efforts and comply with MPA regulations.

Marine tourism and recreation, when carefully managed, serve as powerful drivers of sustainable development. They showcase the economic value of healthy ecosystems, generate jobs, and promote cultural exchange while reinforcing the importance of conservation. By linking ecological protection with economic opportunity, MPAs and sustainable tourism together contribute to the long-term goals of the Blue Economy.

Employment and Livelihood Opportunities

Employment and livelihood opportunities are central to the vision of the Blue Economy, which seeks to align economic growth with environmental sustainability and social equity. Oceans and coasts already support the livelihoods of millions of people worldwide through activities such as fisheries, aquaculture, shipping, tourism, and energy production. MPAs, when effectively designed and managed, strengthen these opportunities by conserving the ecosystems that underpin economic activity while also creating new forms of employment linked to conservation, monitoring, and sustainable industries.

Traditional sectors such as fisheries remain vital sources of employment in many coastal and island communities. Sustainable fisheries management, supported by MPAs, helps maintain fish populations at healthy levels, ensuring that jobs in artisanal and commercial fishing can continue into the future. By protecting spawning grounds and critical habitats, MPAs contribute to replenished stocks that spill over into adjacent areas, supporting both ecological resilience and economic security. This ecological foundation provides stability for livelihoods that might otherwise collapse under the strain of overfishing and environmental degradation.

Tourism and recreation represent another major area of employment linked to marine ecosystems. Well-managed MPAs often become destinations for ecotourism, drawing visitors interested in snorkeling, diving, wildlife watching, and cultural experiences.

Tourism creates jobs in guiding, hospitality, transport, and retail, offering diverse income streams for local communities. Importantly, these jobs often require maintaining healthy ecosystems, creating incentives for residents and businesses to support conservation. By reinvesting tourism revenues into local infrastructure and community projects, MPAs can also stimulate broader economic development beyond tourism alone.

MPAs generate direct employment in conservation and management. Positions such as park rangers, scientists, enforcement officers, and environmental educators are created to support the governance of protected areas. These jobs require skills in monitoring, enforcement, ecological research, and community engagement, contributing to the development of human capital. Capacity-building programs and training initiatives associated with MPAs help equip local residents with the skills needed to participate in these new forms of employment, enhancing resilience and long-term opportunity.

Emerging sectors of the Blue Economy, such as marine renewable energy and biotechnology, also create livelihoods that can benefit from the ecosystem services maintained by MPAs. For example, protecting coastal ecosystems that stabilize shorelines provides secure locations for infrastructure development. Similarly, conserving genetic diversity within MPAs supports future opportunities for marine biotechnology, which depends on access to novel organisms and compounds. By ensuring ecological stability, MPAs indirectly contribute to the growth of these innovative industries.

Community-based livelihood initiatives linked to MPAs further expand opportunities. In many regions, local groups are engaged in activities such as habitat restoration, eco-tourism enterprises, or sustainable aquaculture projects. These initiatives create income streams while reinforcing stewardship of marine resources. By aligning conservation with local economic interests, MPAs foster a sense of ownership and responsibility that strengthens compliance and long-term sustainability.

Employment and livelihood opportunities derived from MPAs highlight the potential for conservation and development to reinforce one another. Rather than restricting economic activity, MPAs create conditions that sustain traditional jobs, diversify income sources, and foster new opportunities in sustainable industries. By linking ecological health with social and economic well-being, MPAs contribute directly to the broader objectives of the Blue Economy, ensuring that people and nature can thrive together.

Balancing Conservation and Development Goals

Balancing conservation and development goals is one of the central challenges of marine governance and a defining feature of the Blue Economy. Oceans provide immense ecological, social, and economic benefits, but competing demands for resources and space often create tensions between protecting biodiversity and promoting economic growth. MPAs sit at the heart of this balancing act. They are designed to conserve ecosystems and species, yet they must also account for the economic needs and cultural practices of human communities that depend on marine resources for their survival. Achieving this balance requires integrated planning, inclusive governance, and adaptive management strategies.

Conservation goals in MPAs focus on preserving biodiversity, safeguarding habitats, and maintaining ecosystem services. These objectives are essential for sustaining the health of marine systems, which in turn underpin long-term economic opportunities. For example, protecting coral reefs helps maintain fish stocks, supports tourism, and provides coastal protection. Similarly, conserving mangroves and seagrass beds enhances carbon sequestration and strengthens resilience against climate change. Without conservation, the ecological foundation of the Blue Economy would be eroded, undermining both current and future development prospects.

On the other hand, development goals emphasize the need to generate livelihoods, foster economic growth, and ensure social equity. Many coastal and island communities rely heavily on marine resources for food, employment, and income. Strictly protected MPAs that limit access to these resources can create economic hardships if alternative opportunities are not available. For this reason, development objectives are often integrated into MPA management, allowing sustainable fishing, ecotourism, and other low-impact activities that contribute to local economies. By embedding sustainable use into MPA frameworks, governments and communities can align development with conservation rather than treating them as opposing forces.

MSP offers a pathway to balance conservation and development. By coordinating different uses of marine space, MSP ensures that MPAs are placed in areas of high ecological value while directing more intensive economic activities to less sensitive areas. Zoning within MPAs also helps reconcile competing objectives. For example, no-take zones may be designated in critical habitats, while multiple-use zones allow for controlled fishing or tourism. This flexible approach enables conservation and development to coexist within the same geographic framework.

Inclusive governance is another cornerstone of achieving balance. Engaging stakeholders such as local communities, fishers, tourism operators, and conservation groups ensures that diverse perspectives are considered in decision-making. Co-management arrangements, where responsibilities are shared between governments and communities, foster ownership and reduce conflicts. By giving stakeholders a role in shaping rules and practices, MPAs can deliver both ecological outcomes and social benefits.

Adaptive management further strengthens the ability to balance goals. Because marine environments and human needs are dynamic, management strategies must evolve in response to new information and changing conditions. Regular monitoring and evaluation help managers adjust regulations, expand or modify zones, and introduce new livelihood initiatives as needed. This flexibility ensures that MPAs remain effective while responding to social and economic realities.

Balancing conservation and development goals is not about compromise that weakens both sides but about integration that reinforces them. Well-managed MPAs demonstrate that conservation can sustain fisheries, tourism, and coastal protection, while sustainable economic activities provide incentives and resources for conservation. By aligning ecological protection with human prosperity, MPAs illustrate how the Blue Economy can achieve its dual objectives of environmental sustainability and inclusive growth.

Chapter 5: Financing the Blue Economy and MPAs

Sustaining the Blue Economy and ensuring the long-term effectiveness of MPAs requires reliable and innovative financing. Traditional public funding alone is often insufficient to meet conservation and management needs, making diverse financial mechanisms essential. This chapter examines the spectrum of financing options, from government budgets and international assistance to innovative instruments such as blue bonds, payment for ecosystem services, and private sector partnerships. It highlights how financial strategies can be designed to ensure sustainability, equity, and accountability, enabling MPAs to deliver ecological, social, and economic benefits well into the future.

Public Funding and Budget Allocations

Public funding and budget allocations are central to the establishment and long-term management of MPAs. While MPAs generate significant ecological, social, and economic benefits, their effectiveness depends on sustained financial support. Governments play a crucial role by allocating resources for planning, implementation, enforcement, monitoring, and community engagement. Without reliable public investment, MPAs risk becoming "paper parks" that exist only in legislation but lack the capacity to deliver meaningful conservation outcomes.

One of the primary uses of public funding is the initial designation and establishment of MPAs. This includes scientific assessments to identify priority areas, stakeholder consultations, and the development of legal frameworks. These processes require technical expertise and administrative resources that are often financed by national budgets. Strong upfront investment ensures that MPAs are grounded in scientific evidence, socially acceptable, and legally enforceable.

Operational costs represent another major area of public expenditure. Effective MPAs require regular patrolling, monitoring of ecological health, and enforcement of regulations. Funding supports personnel such as rangers, scientists, and managers, as well as the equipment and infrastructure needed to carry out their work. For large or remote MPAs, these costs can be substantial, highlighting the need for consistent budgetary commitments rather than short-term project-based financing. Adequate operational budgets are essential to ensure that conservation objectives are achieved and sustained over time.

Public funding is also critical for community engagement and livelihood support. Many coastal and island communities depend heavily on marine resources, and the establishment of MPAs can affect their access to traditional fishing grounds or other economic activities. Allocating resources for education, alternative livelihoods, and participatory governance helps build local support and reduces potential conflicts. By investing in social programs alongside ecological management, governments ensure that MPAs contribute to both conservation and social equity.

Research and monitoring are additional areas that depend on public investment. MPAs require long-term data collection to evaluate their effectiveness, adapt management strategies, and report progress toward national and international biodiversity targets. Universities, research institutes, and government agencies often rely on public budgets to conduct this work. By funding science and monitoring, governments not only ensure accountability but also strengthen the knowledge base for adaptive management.

Budget allocations for MPAs are often justified by the long-term economic returns they generate. Healthy ecosystems provide services such as fisheries productivity, coastal protection, carbon sequestration, and tourism opportunities, all of which reduce public expenditures in other areas. For example, conserving mangroves within MPAs can lower the need for costly artificial coastal defenses, while sustaining fish stocks reduces the risk of economic losses in the fishing industry. Public investment in MPAs can therefore be viewed as preventative spending that saves money over time by reducing environmental degradation and disaster risks.

However, many governments face budgetary constraints and competing priorities, leading to chronic underfunding of MPAs. This highlights the importance of integrating MPA financing into broader national planning frameworks and ensuring that budget allocations are long-term and stable. Linking MPA budgets to climate adaptation, disaster risk reduction, and sustainable development goals can also help secure greater political and financial support.

Public funding and budget allocations are not just about maintaining protected areas—they are investments in ecological resilience, food security, and economic sustainability. By prioritizing MPAs within national budgets, governments demonstrate commitment to protecting marine ecosystems while supporting the livelihoods and well-being of their citizens.

Blue Bonds and Innovative Financing Instruments

Blue bonds and other innovative financing instruments have emerged as important mechanisms for securing sustainable funding for marine conservation and the development of the Blue Economy. Traditional public budgets are often insufficient to cover the costs of establishing and managing MPAs, monitoring marine ecosystems, and supporting community livelihoods. Innovative financial tools provide alternative and complementary sources of funding that mobilize capital from private investors, international institutions, and philanthropic organizations. By linking financial returns to environmental outcomes, these instruments align economic incentives with conservation goals.

Blue bonds are debt instruments specifically designed to raise funds for ocean-related projects, including MPAs, sustainable fisheries, and marine ecosystem restoration. Modeled after green bonds, they provide investors with an opportunity to support environmentally responsible projects while receiving a financial return. Governments, development banks, or corporations issue these bonds, with the proceeds earmarked for sustainable marine initiatives. The Seychelles pioneered this approach in 2018 with the issuance of the world's first sovereign blue bond, which directed funding toward fisheries management and marine conservation. Since then, blue bonds have gained attention as scalable tools to finance marine sustainability.

The appeal of blue bonds lies in their ability to attract a wide range of investors by combining financial security with positive environmental impact. Many are backed by guarantees from international financial institutions, which reduce risk and make them more attractive to investors. This blending of public and private finance helps overcome barriers that often limit investment in conservation, such as uncertainty about returns or the long-term nature of ecological outcomes. By structuring repayment around sustainable resource use or ecosystem services, blue bonds create a direct link between conservation success and financial stability.

In addition to blue bonds, other innovative financing instruments are increasingly being used. Debt-for-nature swaps, for example, restructure a portion of a country's debt in exchange for commitments to invest in conservation. Several coastal and island nations have pursued such agreements to channel funds into marine protection while also improving fiscal sustainability. These swaps free up financial resources that would otherwise go toward debt servicing and redirect them into long-term environmental programs.

Payment for ecosystem services (PES) is another approach that can support MPAs. Under PES schemes, beneficiaries of ecosystem services—such as fisheries, tourism operators, or carbon markets—make payments to support the conservation activities that sustain those services. For instance, dive operators may contribute fees toward reef protection, or carbon credits from blue carbon ecosystems like mangroves can be sold to fund their preservation. By monetizing the value of ecosystem services, PES creates ongoing funding streams that support both conservation and community livelihoods.

Philanthropic partnerships and impact investing also contribute to innovative financing. Foundations and private investors are increasingly interested in funding marine projects that generate both ecological and social benefits. Impact investment funds, for example, target projects that provide measurable conservation outcomes alongside financial returns, such as sustainable aquaculture ventures or coastal restoration initiatives.

Blue bonds and innovative financing instruments diversify the funding base for marine conservation, reducing reliance on limited public budgets. They also create incentives for governments and private actors to integrate sustainability into economic planning. By leveraging financial markets and aligning them with conservation goals, these instruments help ensure that MPAs and the broader Blue Economy have the resources necessary to succeed in the long term.

Private Sector Investments and Partnerships

Private sector investments and partnerships are increasingly recognized as vital to advancing marine conservation and the Blue Economy. While governments and international organizations play central roles in establishing MPAs and developing policy frameworks, the scale of investment required to maintain healthy oceans far exceeds what public funding alone can provide. Engaging businesses, industries, and private investors expands the financial and technical resources available for sustainable ocean management while creating opportunities for innovation and shared responsibility.

One of the most significant contributions the private sector makes is through direct investment in sustainable industries. Sectors such as sustainable fisheries, aquaculture, renewable marine energy, and ecotourism offer clear opportunities for businesses to generate profits while promoting environmental stewardship. For example, companies investing in responsible aquaculture practices reduce pressure on wild fish stocks while creating jobs and income in coastal communities. Similarly, tourism operators benefit from pristine marine environments, making them natural allies in conserving MPAs. By embedding sustainability into their business models, private sector actors align long-term profitability with conservation outcomes.

Partnerships between the private sector and governments or conservation organizations further enhance the effectiveness of MPAs. Corporate partnerships can provide funding, technology, and expertise to support monitoring, enforcement, and habitat restoration. For example, technology firms may supply satellite imaging, drones, or data analytics tools to improve surveillance of illegal fishing within MPAs. Tourism companies often contribute resources for reef restoration projects or education campaigns, recognizing that their success depends on the health of marine ecosystems. These partnerships extend the reach of public agencies and increase the overall capacity for marine protection.

Corporate social responsibility (CSR) initiatives are another channel through which private sector investments support marine conservation. Many businesses, particularly those with direct or indirect reliance on marine resources, allocate CSR funds to conservation programs, community development projects, or awareness campaigns. These initiatives demonstrate corporate commitment to sustainability while delivering tangible benefits to ecosystems and communities. When linked with MPAs, CSR programs can enhance local engagement, improve compliance with conservation rules, and provide additional funding streams.

Impact investing is a growing trend in which private investors seek not only financial returns but also measurable social and environmental benefits. In the marine sector, impact investors fund projects such as sustainable seafood certification, mangrove restoration, or marine renewable energy initiatives. These investments create long-term revenue streams while delivering conservation outcomes, demonstrating that profitability and sustainability are not mutually exclusive.

Public–private partnerships (PPPs) represent a formalized approach to collaboration. In PPPs, governments and private entities share responsibilities for financing, developing, and managing projects that contribute to the Blue Economy. This model has been applied in areas such as sustainable port development, renewable energy infrastructure, and ecotourism facilities, where both sectors benefit from joint investment and risk-sharing. When designed with strong safeguards, PPPs can generate economic growth while ensuring that marine ecosystems remain protected.

Private sector involvement also brings innovation and efficiency to marine management. Businesses often have greater flexibility and resources to experiment with new technologies, market-based incentives, and financial mechanisms. Their participation can help bridge gaps in traditional funding models and accelerate the adoption of sustainable practices.

Private sector investments and partnerships are therefore critical to scaling up marine conservation and ensuring the long-term viability of the Blue Economy. By linking financial interests with ecological sustainability, businesses and investors become active participants in ocean stewardship, complementing public initiatives and helping secure a resilient future for both people and the planet.

Payment for Ecosystem Services

PES is an innovative financing mechanism that links the ecological benefits provided by marine ecosystems to the people and organizations who depend on them. The principle of PES is straightforward: those who benefit from ecosystem services make direct payments to those who manage or conserve the ecosystems that provide them. This approach creates financial incentives for conservation, ensuring that protecting marine and coastal environments becomes economically viable for communities, businesses, and governments. When applied to MPAs, PES helps sustain biodiversity and ecosystem functions while supporting the livelihoods of those who act as stewards of the ocean.

Marine ecosystems provide a wide range of services that often go unrecognized in traditional markets. Coral reefs protect coastlines from erosion and storm surges, mangroves sequester carbon and stabilize shorelines, seagrass beds filter water and support fisheries, and healthy fish stocks contribute to food security. These benefits are enjoyed by coastal communities, industries, and society at large. However, without explicit recognition of their value, there is little incentive to conserve them, leading to degradation and loss. PES addresses this gap by assigning value to ecosystem services and establishing mechanisms for beneficiaries to compensate those who maintain them.

One of the most common applications of PES in marine contexts is in tourism. Tourists pay fees for access to MPAs, diving sites, or wildlife viewing areas, and these funds are reinvested into conservation and management. For example, dive operators may contribute to reef conservation funds, ensuring that coral habitats remain healthy and attractive. This system not only sustains the tourism industry but also provides ongoing revenue for conservation activities. PES in tourism demonstrates how users of ecosystem services can directly support their maintenance.

Another important area for PES is blue carbon. Coastal ecosystems such as mangroves, seagrasses, and salt marshes are highly effective at sequestering carbon dioxide. By quantifying and certifying the carbon storage capacity of these habitats, PES schemes allow governments, companies, or carbon markets to purchase carbon credits that fund their conservation or restoration. This creates dual benefits: reducing greenhouse gas emissions while providing income for local communities engaged in habitat protection. PES for blue carbon is a rapidly growing field with significant potential to finance MPAs.

Fisheries management also offers opportunities for PES. Sustainable certification programs, where consumers pay premiums for sustainably caught seafood, create market-based incentives for fishers to adopt conservation-friendly practices. Similarly, compensation schemes may be developed where downstream beneficiaries, such as commercial fishers, contribute to the conservation of upstream habitats like mangroves that support fish nurseries. These arrangements highlight the interconnectedness of marine ecosystems and the value of collaborative investment in their protection.

For PES schemes to be effective, strong governance and accountability mechanisms are essential. Clear property or usage rights must be established to determine who is entitled to receive payments. Transparent monitoring and reporting systems ensure that funds are used appropriately and that conservation outcomes are achieved. Community participation is also critical, as involving local residents strengthens compliance and ensures that benefits are shared equitably.

Payment for Ecosystem Services transforms conservation from a cost into an investment. By linking financial incentives to ecological stewardship, PES ensures that the benefits of marine ecosystems are recognized, rewarded, and sustained. When integrated with MPAs and broader Blue Economy strategies, PES helps secure both environmental protection and economic opportunity, creating a pathway toward sustainable ocean governance.

International Development Assistance and Philanthropy

International development assistance and philanthropy are vital sources of support for marine conservation and the Blue Economy, particularly in low- and middle-income countries where national budgets are often insufficient to finance MPAs and broader ocean governance initiatives. These funding streams help bridge financial gaps, strengthen institutional capacity, and catalyze innovative projects that protect biodiversity, sustain livelihoods, and build resilience to global challenges such as climate change. By mobilizing resources across borders, development partners and philanthropic organizations play a crucial role in ensuring that marine conservation is not limited by national economic constraints.

Development assistance from multilateral and bilateral donors has long supported marine conservation initiatives. Institutions such as the World Bank, the Global Environment Facility (GEF), and regional development banks provide grants and loans for projects that establish MPAs, enhance fisheries management, and restore coastal ecosystems. Bilateral donors, including agencies from the European Union, the United States, Japan, and other countries, also finance marine programs through targeted aid. These funds often cover essential activities such as scientific research, capacity building, enforcement, and infrastructure development, enabling countries to implement their international commitments under conventions like the Convention on Biological Diversity and the Sustainable Development Goals.

International development assistance is especially important for countries with extensive coastlines but limited resources, such as small island developing states (SIDS). These nations often face disproportionate challenges from overfishing, pollution, and climate impacts yet lack the financial and technical means to address them. Donor-funded projects provide access to expertise, technology, and capital, allowing these states to establish large-scale MPAs, implement marine spatial planning, and develop sustainable ocean-based economies. Development assistance also facilitates regional cooperation, helping neighboring countries coordinate efforts to protect migratory species, shared ecosystems, and transboundary waters.

Philanthropy has become a powerful complement to development assistance, with foundations and charitable organizations funding innovative approaches to marine conservation. Major philanthropic initiatives, such as those by the Pew Charitable Trusts, the Gordon and Betty Moore Foundation, and Bloomberg Philanthropies, have supported the creation of some of the world's largest MPAs. These organizations bring not only financial resources but also advocacy, technical expertise, and global networks that amplify the impact of conservation projects. Philanthropy is often more flexible than traditional aid, allowing for experimentation with new tools, rapid responses to emerging challenges, and long-term commitments to conservation goals.

Philanthropic support also plays a key role in building partnerships between governments, civil society, and local communities. Many foundations fund community-based initiatives that align conservation with local development, such as ecotourism enterprises, sustainable aquaculture projects, or education programs. By empowering communities to participate in conservation, philanthropy strengthens the social foundations of MPAs and ensures that conservation outcomes are both equitable and durable.

Both development assistance and philanthropy can also act as catalysts for additional financing. By demonstrating successful models and reducing initial risks, they encourage private sector investments, impact funding, and innovative mechanisms such as blue bonds or payment for ecosystem services. Blended finance approaches, where philanthropic or donor funding is combined with commercial investment, are increasingly used to scale up marine projects while ensuring sustainability.

International development assistance and philanthropy therefore provide more than just financial resources—they foster innovation, build capacity, and mobilize global solidarity for ocean stewardship. By complementing national budgets and private investments, they ensure that MPAs and marine conservation are adequately supported, enabling countries to pursue both ecological protection and sustainable development within the framework of the Blue Economy.

Chapter 6: Technological Innovations for Sustainable Ocean Management

Technological innovation is transforming the way oceans are managed and conserved, offering powerful tools to enhance the effectiveness of MPAs and the wider Blue Economy. Advances in satellite monitoring, remote sensing, artificial intelligence, and data analytics provide unprecedented insights into marine ecosystems and human activities. These technologies strengthen enforcement, improve decision-making, and support sustainable industries that depend on healthy oceans. This chapter explores the role of emerging technologies in ocean governance, highlighting their potential to increase efficiency, transparency, and resilience while ensuring that conservation and economic objectives are achieved in tandem.

Marine Monitoring and Surveillance Systems

Marine monitoring and surveillance systems are essential tools for the effective management of MPAs and the sustainable use of ocean resources within the Blue Economy. These systems provide the information and enforcement capacity needed to ensure that conservation rules are respected, illegal activities are curtailed, and ecosystems remain healthy. Without monitoring and surveillance, MPAs risk becoming ineffective "paper parks," where regulations exist on paper but are not implemented in practice. Advances in technology, combined with community participation, have transformed how marine environments are observed and protected, making monitoring a cornerstone of modern ocean governance.

Monitoring systems are designed to track ecological, environmental, and socio-economic conditions within and around MPAs. Ecological monitoring focuses on species populations, habitat health, and biodiversity levels, providing critical data on whether conservation objectives are being achieved. For example, tracking fish stocks or coral reef cover helps managers assess the effectiveness of no-take zones. Environmental monitoring captures information on water quality, pollution, and oceanographic conditions, which are essential for detecting emerging threats such as algal blooms or rising sea temperatures. Socio-economic monitoring evaluates the impacts of MPAs on local livelihoods, tourism, and community well-being, ensuring that conservation aligns with development goals.

Surveillance systems, in contrast, are primarily concerned with detecting and deterring illegal or unsustainable activities. These include unauthorized fishing, unregulated shipping, habitat destruction, and wildlife trafficking. Traditional surveillance methods, such as patrols by boats or aircraft, remain important but are often limited by high costs and logistical challenges, especially in large or remote MPAs. New technologies are increasingly used to enhance surveillance capacity and improve cost-effectiveness.

One of the most significant technological advances is satellite-based monitoring. Systems such as Automatic Identification Systems (AIS) and Vessel Monitoring Systems (VMS) allow authorities to track vessel movements in near real-time. By analyzing patterns, managers can detect illegal fishing or unauthorized entry into protected zones. Remote sensing technologies also provide valuable information on habitat changes, such as coral bleaching or mangrove loss, which can be integrated into long-term planning and response strategies.

Unmanned aerial vehicles (drones) are another important tool. They can cover wide areas quickly, collect high-resolution imagery, and monitor activities in areas that are difficult or dangerous for human patrols. Drones are particularly effective for detecting small vessels or monitoring sensitive habitats such as shallow reefs and coastal wetlands. Combined with artificial intelligence and machine learning, these technologies enable rapid data analysis and decision-making.

Community-based monitoring complements high-tech approaches by engaging local stakeholders directly in conservation. Fishers, divers, and community members can collect ecological data, report illegal activities, and participate in enforcement. This approach not only expands monitoring capacity but also builds trust and ownership among communities, ensuring that conservation rules are respected. In many regions, community involvement has proven to be highly effective in reducing illegal fishing and enhancing compliance with MPA regulations.

Integration of monitoring and surveillance systems is critical for success. Effective governance requires coordination between technologies, institutions, and communities to create comprehensive systems that track ecological outcomes, detect violations, and respond promptly. International cooperation also plays a role, particularly in monitoring activities in the high seas where jurisdictional challenges are significant.

Marine monitoring and surveillance systems thus serve as the backbone of MPA management. By combining science, technology, and community engagement, they ensure that conservation objectives are achieved while supporting the sustainable development goals of the Blue Economy. Robust monitoring not only safeguards biodiversity but also provides the data and accountability necessary for long-term ocean stewardship.

Remote Sensing and Satellite Technologies

Remote sensing and satellite technologies have become indispensable for modern marine conservation and management. In the context of the Blue Economy and MPAs, these tools provide cost-effective, large-scale, and continuous data collection that would otherwise be impossible to achieve using only traditional field methods. By offering real-time insights into ecological conditions, human activities, and environmental change, remote sensing supports decision-making, enhances enforcement, and strengthens the capacity to balance conservation and sustainable development goals.

One of the primary applications of remote sensing in marine environments is habitat monitoring. High-resolution satellite imagery allows scientists and managers to map and track ecosystems such as coral reefs, mangroves, seagrass beds, and coastal wetlands. These habitats are critical for biodiversity, fisheries, and climate regulation but are often under threat from development, pollution, and climate change. Satellite data can reveal changes in habitat extent and health over time, enabling early detection of degradation. For example, coral bleaching events can be monitored through satellites that measure sea surface temperature and light reflectance, providing timely alerts for managers.

Remote sensing also plays a vital role in monitoring oceanographic conditions. Satellites track sea surface temperature, chlorophyll concentrations, salinity, sea level rise, and ocean currents—parameters essential for understanding the dynamics of marine ecosystems. This information helps predict ecological shifts, such as changes in fish distribution driven by warming waters, and informs adaptive management strategies. In MPAs, oceanographic data can guide zoning, enforcement, and the design of ecological networks that account for species movements and environmental variability.

Surveillance of human activity is another crucial function of satellite technology. Tools such as AIS and VMS, integrated with satellite platforms, allow authorities to track the movement of vessels across oceans. This is especially valuable for detecting illegal, unreported, and unregulated (IUU) fishing, which undermines conservation and food security. By overlaying vessel data with MPA boundaries, managers can identify violations in near real-time and take enforcement action. Satellite technologies therefore extend the reach of enforcement far beyond what traditional patrols can achieve.

Advances in remote sensing are increasingly linked with artificial intelligence (AI) and machine learning. These technologies enable the rapid processing of vast datasets, identifying patterns and anomalies that would be difficult to detect manually. For instance, AI-driven analysis of satellite imagery can distinguish between different types of fishing vessels, detect habitat changes, or forecast areas at risk of illegal activity. By automating data interpretation, these systems make monitoring more efficient and accessible to resource-limited agencies.

Remote sensing also supports transparency and accountability. Many satellite datasets are publicly available and can be used by civil society, researchers, and local communities to monitor activities in marine areas. Initiatives such as Global Fishing Watch provide open access to vessel tracking data, empowering stakeholders to hold governments and industries accountable. This democratization of information strengthens governance by creating shared responsibility for ocean stewardship.

Finally, remote sensing and satellite technologies are critical for addressing global challenges such as climate change. They provide the long-term datasets needed to understand trends in ocean warming, acidification, and sea level rise, and they inform international agreements and national policies. By integrating these tools into marine governance, MPAs and the wider Blue Economy benefit from science-based, adaptive, and resilient management.

Remote sensing and satellite technologies therefore act as powerful enablers of marine conservation. By bridging ecological knowledge, enforcement capacity, and community participation, they enhance the effectiveness of MPAs and ensure that the Blue Economy develops on a foundation of sustainability and accountability.

Data Analytics and Decision Support Tools

Data analytics and decision support tools have become essential in the management of MPAs and the broader Blue Economy. As oceans generate vast amounts of ecological, environmental, and socio-economic data, the ability to process, analyze, and apply this information is critical for effective governance. By turning raw data into actionable insights, analytics and decision support systems help managers set priorities, allocate resources, and adapt strategies to changing conditions, ensuring that conservation and development objectives are met simultaneously.

One of the primary roles of data analytics in marine governance is ecological monitoring. MPAs generate data on species abundance, habitat health, water quality, and ecosystem interactions. Advanced analytical techniques allow managers to detect trends, identify stressors, and measure the success of conservation interventions. For example, statistical modeling and machine learning can reveal correlations between fishing pressure and fish stock recovery, or between sea surface temperature and coral bleaching. These insights provide evidence for adjusting management measures such as catch limits, zoning rules, or restoration efforts.

Decision support tools translate this analytical capacity into practical management frameworks. Geographic Information Systems (GIS), for instance, enable managers to visualize spatial data on ecosystems, human activities, and threats. By overlaying multiple datasets, GIS helps identify areas of high ecological value, conflict hotspots between conservation and development, or regions where MPAs could be expanded. Scenario modeling within GIS allows policymakers to test different management options—such as stricter fishing controls, tourism zoning, or habitat restoration—and assess their ecological and economic impacts before implementation.

Data analytics is also critical for managing human activities within and around MPAs. VMS, AIS, and other tracking technologies produce vast streams of movement data. Analytical platforms process these data to detect IUU fishing, monitor compliance with MPA regulations, and predict areas at risk of future violations. Decision support dashboards provide managers with real-time alerts and evidence-based recommendations for enforcement actions, significantly improving efficiency and reducing costs.

Socio-economic data adds another important dimension. Understanding how MPAs affect livelihoods, tourism, and community well-being ensures that conservation measures are socially sustainable. Data analytics can reveal whether local fishers benefit from spillover effects, whether tourism revenues are equitably distributed, or whether communities face economic displacement. Decision support systems that integrate ecological and socio-economic data help managers strike a balance between conservation goals and human needs, reducing conflicts and fostering community support.

Adaptive management relies heavily on these tools. Because marine ecosystems and human activities are dynamic, managers must constantly update strategies in response to new information. Data-driven platforms facilitate this by providing feedback loops: monitoring results are analyzed, recommendations are generated, and management plans are adjusted accordingly. This iterative process enhances resilience and ensures that MPAs remain effective under changing environmental and socio-economic conditions, including those driven by climate change.

Collaborative platforms further expand the impact of data analytics. Cloud-based decision support tools allow governments, NGOs, researchers, and local communities to share data and insights, improving coordination and transparency. Open-access platforms also empower civil society to participate in monitoring and advocacy, strengthening accountability in marine governance.

Data analytics and decision support tools are therefore central to modern marine management. By transforming complex datasets into clear, actionable knowledge, they enable evidence-based decisions that support both biodiversity conservation and sustainable economic development. In doing so, they help secure the ecological and social foundations of the Blue Economy.

Innovations in Sustainable Marine Industries

Innovations in sustainable marine industries are reshaping the way societies interact with the ocean, providing new opportunities for economic growth while reducing ecological pressures. As the Blue Economy evolves, technological advancements and creative business models are enabling industries to align profitability with conservation. From fisheries and aquaculture to renewable energy and biotechnology, innovations are helping to ensure that marine resources are harnessed in ways that sustain biodiversity, support livelihoods, and build resilience against climate change.

Sustainable fisheries have been at the forefront of marine innovation. Traditional fishing practices have often led to overexploitation, but new technologies and management systems are reversing this trend. Electronic monitoring devices, blockchain traceability systems, and eco-certification programs allow consumers and regulators to track seafood from ocean to plate, ensuring transparency and compliance with sustainability standards. Gear innovations, such as selective nets that reduce bycatch, also contribute to healthier fish stocks and marine ecosystems. These tools create market advantages for responsible fishers, while ensuring that conservation and food security goals are met.

Aquaculture, one of the fastest-growing food sectors globally, is also experiencing transformative innovations. Sustainable aquaculture systems include offshore farming platforms, recirculating aquaculture systems (RAS), and integrated multi-trophic aquaculture (IMTA). Offshore farms reduce pressure on coastal habitats, while RAS minimizes water use and pollution by recycling water in controlled environments. IMTA, which combines species such as fish, shellfish, and seaweed, mimics natural ecosystems and maximizes efficiency by turning waste from one species into resources for another. These innovations reduce environmental impacts while expanding food production in line with rising demand.

Marine renewable energy represents another key area of innovation. Offshore wind farms are rapidly expanding, providing clean energy that reduces reliance on fossil fuels. Wave and tidal energy technologies are advancing as well, offering additional renewable options with the potential to power coastal communities. Innovations in energy storage and grid integration are making these technologies more reliable and scalable. By harnessing marine energy, countries can meet climate goals while creating jobs and reducing ecological pressures associated with traditional energy systems.

The biotechnology sector is also driving sustainable marine innovation. Marine organisms, from algae to sponges, are sources of valuable compounds for pharmaceuticals, cosmetics, and nutraceuticals. Advances in marine biotechnology allow for the sustainable harvesting or cultivation of these organisms, reducing reliance on wild populations. Seaweed farming, in particular, has gained global attention as a sustainable industry with multiple benefits: it absorbs carbon dioxide, improves water quality, and provides raw materials for food, biofuels, and biodegradable packaging. This sector exemplifies how marine industries can generate economic value while contributing to climate mitigation and ecosystem health.

Tourism is also being reshaped by innovation, with eco-tourism and digital platforms creating opportunities for sustainable marine experiences. Virtual reality (VR) and augmented reality (AR) are being used to promote marine awareness and reduce physical pressure on sensitive ecosystems. Smart technologies also allow operators to manage visitor flows more sustainably, ensuring that tourism supports conservation while providing economic benefits.

Innovations in sustainable marine industries demonstrate that environmental stewardship and economic growth are not mutually exclusive. By combining cutting-edge technologies, sustainable practices, and inclusive governance, these industries are paving the way for a Blue Economy that delivers prosperity while safeguarding ocean health. Their success underscores the importance of innovation as a driving force in building a sustainable and resilient future for marine ecosystems and human societies.

Role of Emerging Technologies in MPA Management

Emerging technologies are transforming the way MPAs are established, monitored, and managed, making conservation efforts more efficient, transparent, and adaptive. As pressures on the ocean grow from overfishing, climate change, and pollution, traditional management methods are often insufficient to address the scale and complexity of challenges. New tools—including artificial intelligence (AI), drones, satellite systems, blockchain, and advanced sensors—are expanding the capacity of governments, researchers, and communities to safeguard marine ecosystems. By integrating these technologies into governance frameworks, MPAs can achieve stronger conservation outcomes while aligning with the broader goals of the Blue Economy.

Artificial intelligence and machine learning are among the most impactful innovations for MPA management. These tools can process vast datasets from satellites, sensors, and ecological surveys, identifying patterns and anomalies that would be difficult for humans to detect. For instance, AI can distinguish between legal and illegal fishing activities by analyzing vessel movement data from AIS or VMS. Machine learning models also predict coral bleaching events, track changes in fish populations, and forecast ecosystem responses to climate change, enabling managers to act proactively rather than reactively.

Drones, or unmanned aerial vehicles (UAVs), provide another powerful technology for MPA monitoring and enforcement. They can survey large or remote areas at relatively low cost, capturing high-resolution imagery of habitats and human activities. Drones are particularly useful for detecting illegal fishing, monitoring coastal erosion, or assessing the condition of coral reefs and mangroves. Equipped with thermal imaging or multispectral sensors, drones provide detailed ecological data that complement satellite monitoring. Their agility and affordability make them especially valuable for smaller nations or local communities with limited resources.

Satellite technologies remain a cornerstone of emerging tools for MPAs. Advances in remote sensing allow for near real-time monitoring of oceanographic conditions such as sea surface temperature, chlorophyll concentration, and salinity. These data are critical for understanding ecosystem health and detecting climate-related stressors. Satellite-based vessel tracking, combined with platforms like Global Fishing Watch, increases transparency by making fishing activity visible to governments, NGOs, and the public. This open-access approach strengthens accountability and deters IUU fishing, one of the most significant threats to MPAs worldwide.

Blockchain technology is also emerging as a tool for improving transparency and trust in marine resource management. By creating secure, traceable records of transactions, blockchain enables the verification of sustainable seafood supply chains. Fish caught legally within or near MPAs can be tracked from harvest to consumer, ensuring compliance with conservation rules and rewarding sustainable practices. This system empowers both regulators and consumers to support responsible fishing and strengthens the economic incentives for marine stewardship.

Advanced sensor technologies further enhance MPA management by providing real-time data from the ocean itself. Underwater acoustic sensors, for example, track marine mammal activity or detect illegal dynamite fishing. Environmental DNA (eDNA) technologies allow scientists to monitor species presence and abundance by analyzing genetic material in seawater samples, offering a non-invasive and cost-effective way to track biodiversity.

Together, these emerging technologies expand the toolkit available for MPA governance. They improve the precision of monitoring, enhance enforcement capacity, reduce costs, and foster transparency. Importantly, they also empower communities and stakeholders by making information more accessible and actionable. As these technologies continue to evolve, their integration into marine governance will be essential for ensuring that MPAs meet conservation targets while supporting the sustainable development objectives of the Blue Economy.

Chapter 7: Climate Change, MPAs, and Ocean Resilience

Climate change poses one of the greatest threats to marine ecosystems and the communities that depend on them. Rising sea temperatures, ocean acidification, sea level rise, and stronger storms are reshaping marine environments and intensifying pressures on biodiversity. MPAs are increasingly recognized as essential tools for strengthening ocean resilience, safeguarding blue carbon ecosystems, and supporting climate adaptation and mitigation. This chapter examines the links between climate change and MPAs, exploring how protected areas contribute to both ecological stability and human resilience, while aligning with global efforts to address the ocean–climate nexus.

Ocean–Climate Nexus

The ocean–climate nexus highlights the profound interconnections between marine ecosystems and the global climate system. Oceans regulate the Earth's climate by absorbing vast amounts of heat and carbon dioxide, while marine ecosystems such as mangroves, seagrasses, and salt marshes act as vital carbon sinks. At the same time, oceans are increasingly vulnerable to the impacts of climate change, including rising temperatures, ocean acidification, sea level rise, and more frequent extreme weather events. Understanding and addressing this nexus is critical for both marine conservation and global climate resilience, making it central to the Blue Economy and the management of MPAs.

Oceans absorb over 90 percent of the excess heat generated by greenhouse gas emissions and nearly a third of carbon dioxide released into the atmosphere. This buffering capacity reduces the immediate effects of climate change on land but comes at a cost to marine ecosystems. Warmer waters contribute to coral bleaching, disrupt species distributions, and affect the productivity of fisheries. Ocean acidification, caused by the absorption of carbon dioxide, weakens the shells and skeletons of marine organisms such as corals, mollusks, and plankton, undermining the very foundation of marine food webs. These changes threaten biodiversity, ecosystem services, and the livelihoods of millions of people.

MPAs play a crucial role in responding to the challenges of the ocean–climate nexus. By protecting critical habitats such as mangroves, seagrass meadows, and salt marshes, MPAs safeguard "blue carbon" ecosystems that capture and store significant amounts of carbon. Conserving these habitats prevents the release of stored carbon while enhancing their capacity to absorb new emissions. MPAs also support the resilience of marine ecosystems, allowing species and habitats to recover from climate stressors and adapt to changing conditions. Healthy ecosystems are better able to buffer coastal communities from storms, reduce erosion, and maintain fisheries productivity in the face of climate change.

The nexus also highlights the importance of marine biodiversity for climate adaptation. Diverse ecosystems provide multiple functions, from sustaining fisheries to regulating water quality, and are more resilient to environmental change. Protecting biodiversity within MPAs ensures that ecosystems retain their capacity to adapt and continue delivering critical services. For example, preserving coral reef diversity enhances the ability of reefs to recover after bleaching events, while maintaining genetic diversity in fish populations supports adaptation to shifting temperatures and habitats.

Climate change, in turn, requires MPAs to adopt adaptive and forward-looking management strategies. This includes identifying climate refugia—areas less vulnerable to warming or acidification—that can serve as safe havens for species. It also involves designing MPA networks that account for shifting species ranges and ecological connectivity across larger spatial scales. Integrating climate science into marine spatial planning ensures that conservation strategies are robust under future climate scenarios.

The ocean–climate nexus is also deeply linked to global policy frameworks. International agreements such as the Paris Agreement recognize the role of oceans and blue carbon ecosystems in achieving climate goals. Incorporating MPAs and marine conservation into national climate strategies enhances their effectiveness and creates synergies between biodiversity protection and climate mitigation.

By addressing the ocean–climate nexus, societies can achieve dual benefits: protecting marine ecosystems while enhancing global resilience to climate change. Through MPAs and the broader Blue Economy, the nexus is not only a challenge but also an opportunity to align conservation, development, and climate action in pursuit of a sustainable future.

MPAs as Climate Adaptation and Mitigation Tools

MPAs are increasingly recognized not only for their role in biodiversity conservation but also as vital tools for climate adaptation and mitigation. As climate change intensifies pressures on the ocean—through rising temperatures, acidification, sea level rise, and extreme weather events—MPAs provide nature-based solutions that strengthen ecological resilience and support human communities. By conserving critical habitats, enhancing ecosystem services, and storing carbon, MPAs contribute directly to both reducing the causes of climate change and adapting to its impacts, positioning them as key elements of the Blue Economy.

One of the most important contributions of MPAs to climate mitigation is their role in protecting and restoring blue carbon ecosystems. Mangroves, seagrasses, and salt marshes are among the most efficient carbon sinks on the planet, capturing and storing carbon at rates far higher than terrestrial forests. By designating these habitats within MPAs, governments and communities prevent their degradation and the release of stored carbon while maintaining their ongoing sequestration capacity. Restoring degraded blue carbon habitats within MPAs further enhances carbon storage, aligning conservation efforts with global climate commitments such as the Paris Agreement.

Beyond carbon sequestration, MPAs provide adaptation benefits by safeguarding ecosystems that buffer human communities from climate impacts. Coastal habitats such as mangroves and coral reefs reduce wave energy, protect shorelines from erosion, and diminish the impact of storm surges. By maintaining these natural barriers, MPAs reduce the vulnerability of coastal populations to extreme weather events, offering a cost-effective alternative to engineered infrastructure. For small island states and low-lying coastal nations, these protective functions are particularly critical to resilience and survival.

MPAs also enhance the adaptive capacity of marine species and ecosystems. Healthy, diverse ecosystems are more resilient to environmental stressors and better able to recover from disturbances. For example, coral reefs within MPAs that are spared from overfishing and destructive practices show greater recovery after bleaching events. Protecting areas that serve as climate refugia— regions less affected by warming or acidification—ensures that species have safe havens from which they can recolonize affected areas. MPAs designed as networks, rather than isolated sites, further support adaptation by facilitating species migration and genetic exchange across broader ecological landscapes.

For human communities, MPAs contribute to climate adaptation by sustaining livelihoods and food security under changing conditions. By protecting fish breeding grounds and nursery habitats, MPAs help maintain fish populations that are critical sources of protein for millions of people. The spillover effect from MPAs into adjacent fishing areas supports fisheries even as climate change alters species distributions. Additionally, MPAs that promote sustainable tourism or aquaculture provide diversified livelihood opportunities, reducing economic vulnerability in the face of climate shocks.

Integrating climate considerations into MPA planning is essential to maximize these benefits. Adaptive management strategies must account for future scenarios, shifting species ranges, and changing ocean conditions. Linking MPAs with national climate policies, disaster risk reduction strategies, and international climate finance mechanisms strengthens their role as dual-purpose tools for conservation and climate action.

Marine Protected Areas thus serve as powerful instruments for both mitigating climate change and adapting to its effects. By conserving ecosystems that store carbon, protect coasts, and sustain biodiversity, MPAs reduce risks, build resilience, and contribute to a sustainable ocean economy. In doing so, they embody the principle that protecting nature is not only an environmental imperative but also a practical and effective strategy for addressing the global climate crisis.

Protecting Blue Carbon Ecosystems

Protecting blue carbon ecosystems—mangroves, seagrasses, and salt marshes—is a priority for advancing both marine conservation and global climate action. These coastal habitats are unique in their ability to sequester and store carbon at rates far higher than most terrestrial systems. At the same time, they support biodiversity, sustain fisheries, and protect coastal communities from environmental hazards. Despite their importance, blue carbon ecosystems are disappearing at alarming rates due to development, pollution, and climate pressures. Incorporating these habitats into MPAs provides a powerful mechanism to conserve them and maintain their ecological and socio-economic benefits.

Blue carbon ecosystems are exceptional natural carbon sinks. Mangroves, for instance, not only capture carbon in their above-ground biomass but also in the deep organic-rich soils beneath them, where carbon can remain locked for centuries. Seagrasses and salt marshes perform a similar role, absorbing carbon dioxide and storing it in sediments that accumulate over time. When these ecosystems are degraded or destroyed, stored carbon is released back into the atmosphere, contributing to greenhouse gas emissions. Protecting and restoring them within MPAs prevents these emissions while maintaining their capacity to sequester new carbon, directly linking local conservation to global climate mitigation goals.

Beyond their role in carbon storage, these ecosystems provide significant adaptation benefits for human societies. Mangroves and salt marshes reduce coastal erosion, stabilize shorelines, and dissipate wave energy, acting as natural defenses against storms and rising seas. Seagrasses improve water quality by filtering pollutants and trapping sediments, enhancing the resilience of coral reefs and other marine habitats. These services reduce vulnerability for coastal populations, especially in small island and low-lying nations where exposure to climate hazards is high. Protecting blue carbon ecosystems therefore strengthens resilience to climate change in ways that are both cost-effective and sustainable compared with built infrastructure.

Biodiversity conservation adds another layer of importance. Blue carbon ecosystems provide nursery grounds for fish, crustaceans, and mollusks that sustain commercial and subsistence fisheries. They also serve as feeding and breeding habitats for endangered species, including sea turtles, dugongs, and migratory birds. Safeguarding these habitats within MPAs supports ecological connectivity and helps maintain healthy food webs, which in turn sustain livelihoods and food security for millions of people.

Despite their immense value, blue carbon ecosystems are among the most threatened on Earth. Mangroves continue to be cleared for aquaculture and coastal development, seagrasses are damaged by dredging and pollution, and salt marshes are drained for agriculture or infrastructure. These losses compromise both conservation and climate objectives. MPAs can help reverse these trends by providing legal protection, regulating harmful activities, and supporting large-scale restoration efforts.

Protecting blue carbon ecosystems also opens pathways for innovative financing. Conservation and restoration projects can generate carbon credits, which may be sold in voluntary or compliance markets to fund local management and provide economic benefits to communities. By creating revenue streams tied to ecological stewardship, carbon markets incentivize long-term protection and enhance local engagement in conservation.

Safeguarding blue carbon ecosystems through MPAs reflects the integrated vision of the Blue Economy. These habitats simultaneously capture carbon, buffer climate impacts, sustain biodiversity, and support livelihoods. Protecting them ensures that oceans contribute to both global climate stability and the well-being of coastal societies.

Enhancing Climate Resilience of Coastal Communities

Enhancing the climate resilience of coastal communities is a fundamental goal of the Blue Economy and closely tied to the effective management of MPAs. Coastal populations face disproportionate risks from the impacts of climate change, including sea level rise, coastal erosion, stronger storms, and changing fish stocks. These communities are often highly dependent on marine resources for food, livelihoods, and cultural identity, making them vulnerable to ecological degradation. By conserving critical habitats, supporting sustainable livelihoods, and fostering adaptive governance, MPAs contribute significantly to building resilience for coastal societies.

One of the most important ways MPAs enhance resilience is through the protection of natural coastal defenses. Mangroves, coral reefs, and seagrass beds—all commonly included within MPA boundaries—provide essential ecosystem services that reduce vulnerability to climate hazards. Coral reefs dissipate wave energy, mangroves stabilize shorelines and trap sediments, and seagrasses reduce water turbidity, creating healthier marine conditions. Together, these ecosystems act as buffers against storms, storm surges, and sea level rise, safeguarding lives and infrastructure. Protecting and restoring these habitats reduces the need for expensive engineered defenses, offering a natural and sustainable approach to coastal protection.

MPAs also strengthen resilience by sustaining fisheries that provide both food security and income. Healthy fish populations are essential to the nutrition and economic well-being of coastal communities, particularly in small island states and developing nations. By protecting spawning and nursery grounds, MPAs allow fish stocks to replenish and spill over into adjacent fishing areas, ensuring long-term productivity. This ecological foundation supports resilience by reducing the risk of resource collapse and ensuring communities maintain access to critical food supplies even as climate change alters marine conditions.

Livelihood diversification within MPAs further enhances community resilience. Beyond fishing, MPAs often create opportunities in ecotourism, habitat restoration, and conservation management. Jobs such as park rangers, eco-guides, or monitoring assistants provide alternative sources of income, reducing dependence on a single resource sector vulnerable to climate variability. These new livelihoods not only support economic stability but also build stronger social ties to conservation, as communities see direct benefits from protecting marine ecosystems.

Cultural resilience is another important dimension. For many coastal and island societies, marine ecosystems are deeply tied to cultural identity, heritage, and traditional knowledge. MPAs that integrate community participation and respect cultural practices help preserve these connections, strengthening social cohesion and reinforcing collective capacity to respond to change. Engaging communities in co-management ensures that conservation strategies are locally appropriate and supported, making them more effective over the long term.

Adaptive governance within MPAs is critical to resilience. Climate change introduces uncertainty, and management must evolve in response to new challenges. Regular monitoring, community feedback, and flexible policies allow MPAs to adapt strategies as conditions change. This iterative approach ensures that conservation continues to provide meaningful benefits for ecosystems and people under future climate scenarios.

Enhancing climate resilience through MPAs reflects the integration of ecological, social, and economic strategies. By protecting natural defenses, sustaining food systems, diversifying livelihoods, and empowering communities, MPAs contribute to both immediate safety and long-term adaptation. Coastal communities that benefit from resilient ecosystems are better equipped to withstand and recover from climate impacts, securing their place in a sustainable Blue Economy.

Global Climate Policy Linkages

Global climate policy linkages are increasingly shaping the role of oceans and MPAs in addressing climate change. International frameworks recognize that healthy marine ecosystems are not only vital for biodiversity but also central to climate mitigation and adaptation. By connecting marine conservation with climate policy, governments and international organizations create opportunities to integrate MPAs and blue carbon ecosystems into broader strategies for achieving global climate goals. These linkages highlight the importance of aligning ocean governance with agreements such as the Paris Agreement, the Sustainable Development Goals (SDGs), and biodiversity conventions.

The Paris Agreement represents the most significant global framework for climate action, and while it does not explicitly mention oceans, its mechanisms create pathways to integrate marine conservation. Nationally Determined Contributions (NDCs), the core commitments under the agreement, increasingly include ocean-based strategies such as protecting blue carbon ecosystems, expanding MPAs, and restoring coastal habitats. These actions contribute both to mitigation, through carbon sequestration, and to adaptation, by reducing climate risks to vulnerable communities. Linking MPAs to NDCs ensures that marine conservation is embedded in national climate strategies and supported by international finance and reporting mechanisms.

The CBD also plays a central role in linking climate and marine policy. Through its post-2020 Global Biodiversity Framework, the CBD emphasizes the need to protect at least 30 percent of the planet's land and sea by 2030 ("30x30"). MPAs are a primary tool to achieve this target, and their contribution to climate mitigation and resilience strengthens the connection between biodiversity protection and climate action. By aligning biodiversity and climate goals, the CBD creates synergies that enhance the effectiveness of global policy frameworks.

Blue carbon ecosystems serve as a critical bridge between marine conservation and climate policy. International initiatives, such as the Blue Carbon Initiative and the UN's REDD+ program (Reducing Emissions from Deforestation and Forest Degradation), have expanded to include coastal ecosystems, recognizing their role in carbon storage. By linking carbon markets to the conservation of mangroves, seagrasses, and salt marshes, these frameworks provide opportunities for countries to finance marine conservation through climate mechanisms. This integration underscores the value of MPAs not only for biodiversity but also for achieving emissions reduction targets.

Global climate policy linkages also extend to the Sustainable Development Goals. SDG 13 (Climate Action) and SDG 14 (Life Below Water) are mutually reinforcing, with MPAs contributing to both. By safeguarding ecosystems that provide food, livelihoods, and coastal protection, MPAs support broader development goals such as poverty reduction (SDG 1) and sustainable consumption and production (SDG 12). These interconnections emphasize that climate and marine policies cannot be pursued in isolation but must be addressed through integrated approaches.

International climate finance mechanisms further strengthen linkages between global policy and marine conservation. Funds such as the Green Climate Fund (GCF) and the Global Environment Facility (GEF) support projects that link MPAs to climate mitigation and adaptation objectives. Accessing these funds allows developing countries to expand their MPA networks, restore blue carbon ecosystems, and enhance community resilience, ensuring that conservation is supported by sustainable financing.

Global climate policy linkages demonstrate the increasingly interconnected nature of ocean and climate governance. By embedding MPAs and marine ecosystems within international climate frameworks, the world community recognizes that safeguarding oceans is essential to addressing the climate crisis. These connections not only elevate the role of MPAs in global strategies but also unlock resources, partnerships, and accountability mechanisms that strengthen their impact.

Chapter 8: Integrating MPAs Into the Wider Blue Economy Strategy

MPAs must be understood not as isolated conservation efforts but as integral components of the broader Blue Economy. Their success depends on effective integration with fisheries, tourism, shipping, energy, and other marine-based sectors. This chapter explores how MPAs can be embedded within national and regional strategies through marine spatial planning, ecosystem-based management, sustainable supply chains, and cross-sectoral coordination. It highlights the importance of aligning conservation with development goals, ensuring that MPAs contribute to economic prosperity, social well-being, and ecological integrity as part of a cohesive and forward-looking ocean strategy.

Marine Spatial Planning and Zoning

MSP and zoning are fundamental tools for managing the competing demands placed on ocean space while ensuring the conservation of biodiversity and the sustainable use of marine resources. As part of the Blue Economy framework, MSP provides an integrated, ecosystem-based approach that balances ecological, economic, and social objectives. Within this context, zoning acts as a practical mechanism to allocate specific areas of the ocean for designated uses, including MPAs, fisheries, tourism, shipping, and energy development. Together, MSP and zoning enable governments and stakeholders to reduce conflicts, optimize resource use, and safeguard marine ecosystems.

At its core, MSP is a forward-looking planning process that organizes the spatial and temporal distribution of human activities in marine and coastal areas. Unlike traditional sectoral management, which often addresses one activity at a time, MSP considers multiple sectors and their cumulative impacts. This holistic perspective allows for better alignment between conservation and development goals, ensuring that MPAs are integrated into broader ocean governance strategies rather than managed in isolation. MSP frameworks are particularly important in regions where resource competition is intense, such as coastal zones and archipelagic waters.

Zoning serves as a critical component of MSP by defining how specific areas of the ocean will be used and managed. Within MPAs, zoning often separates areas into categories such as no-take zones, multiple-use areas, and buffer zones. No-take zones, where extractive activities are prohibited, provide strong protection for biodiversity and allow ecosystems to recover and thrive. Multiple-use zones may permit sustainable fishing, tourism, or research under regulated conditions, while buffer zones reduce pressures on core conservation areas. This structured approach ensures that ecological integrity is maintained while still supporting economic activities that contribute to local livelihoods.

Beyond MPAs, zoning also addresses broader spatial conflicts between sectors. For instance, MSP may designate shipping lanes to avoid sensitive habitats, or identify sites for offshore wind farms that minimize impacts on fisheries and wildlife. By carefully allocating space, zoning reduces competition between incompatible activities and enhances overall efficiency. In this way, MSP supports the coexistence of conservation and development, a central objective of the Blue Economy.

MSP and zoning processes rely heavily on data and stakeholder engagement. Ecological data, such as species distribution and habitat maps, are combined with information on economic activities and community needs to create balanced plans. Decision support tools, including GIS, help visualize trade-offs and test different scenarios. Equally important is the involvement of stakeholders—fishers, tourism operators, local communities, conservation groups, and industry representatives—who provide local knowledge and ensure that zoning decisions are socially equitable and widely accepted.

Adaptive management is an essential feature of MSP. Marine ecosystems and human activities are dynamic, and zoning arrangements must evolve in response to new information, environmental change, and shifting societal priorities. Regular monitoring and review allow managers to adjust zoning rules, expand or modify MPAs, and respond to emerging challenges such as climate change and technological development.

Marine Spatial Planning and zoning create a framework where conservation and economic activity reinforce each other rather than compete. By providing clarity, reducing conflict, and ensuring sustainable use, they strengthen the effectiveness of MPAs and enhance resilience in marine governance. As ocean pressures continue to increase, MSP stands out as a key strategy for aligning human aspirations with ecological realities.

Ecosystem-Based Management Approaches

Ecosystem-Based Management (EBM) approaches are central to modern ocean governance, offering a holistic framework that accounts for the complexity and interconnectedness of marine ecosystems. Unlike traditional sectoral management, which often addresses individual resources or activities in isolation, EBM considers entire ecosystems—including ecological processes, human uses, and social dimensions—when making decisions. In the context of the Blue Economy and MPAs, EBM provides a pathway to balance conservation, development, and community well-being, ensuring that marine resources are used sustainably while maintaining ecosystem integrity.

The foundation of EBM is the recognition that ecosystems function as interconnected systems where changes in one component can have cascading effects across others. Overfishing, for instance, not only reduces fish populations but can also alter food webs, degrade habitats, and diminish the resilience of ecosystems to climate change. EBM addresses these linkages by managing human activities in ways that sustain ecological processes, biodiversity, and ecosystem services. This broad perspective makes EBM particularly well-suited to the marine environment, where boundaries are fluid and interactions between species, habitats, and people are highly dynamic.

MPAs are an important tool for implementing EBM, but EBM extends beyond protected areas to encompass entire seascapes. Within MPAs, EBM guides the design of zoning systems, ensuring that no-take zones, multiple-use areas, and buffer zones function together to protect biodiversity while allowing sustainable uses. Beyond MPAs, EBM informs MSP, fisheries management, and pollution control, ensuring that activities across sectors are aligned with ecological sustainability. By integrating MPAs into broader governance frameworks, EBM ensures that conservation is not isolated but embedded within larger socio-ecological systems.

A key element of EBM is the incorporation of ecosystem services into decision-making. Marine ecosystems provide critical services such as food provision, carbon sequestration, coastal protection, and cultural value. EBM ensures that these services are recognized, valued, and maintained. For example, conserving mangroves within an EBM framework supports both biodiversity and climate mitigation through carbon storage, while also protecting communities from storm surges. By highlighting these multiple benefits, EBM strengthens the case for conservation and helps build political and social support for sustainable management.

EBM is also characterized by its emphasis on adaptive management. Marine systems are subject to uncertainty and change, particularly under the pressures of climate change. EBM requires continuous monitoring of ecological and social indicators, evaluation of outcomes, and adjustment of management strategies based on new information. This iterative process allows managers to respond flexibly to emerging threats and opportunities, ensuring that governance remains effective in dynamic environments.

Stakeholder engagement is another cornerstone of EBM. Because ecosystems support diverse human communities and activities, successful management requires inclusive governance that involves fishers, tourism operators, conservation organizations, indigenous peoples, and local residents. By incorporating diverse perspectives and knowledge systems, including traditional and indigenous knowledge, EBM enhances legitimacy, equity, and compliance. Participatory processes also help resolve conflicts, fostering cooperation among stakeholders with different interests.

Ecosystem-Based Management approaches therefore represent a shift from fragmented, short-term resource use to integrated, long-term stewardship. By recognizing the interconnectedness of ecological and human systems, EBM provides a comprehensive strategy for aligning marine conservation with sustainable development. In the context of the Blue Economy, EBM ensures that economic opportunities are pursued without compromising the ecological foundations on which they depend, creating resilient ecosystems and communities alike.

Linking MPAs to Sustainable Supply Chains

Linking MPAs to sustainable supply chains is an increasingly important strategy for aligning ocean conservation with economic development. Supply chains for seafood, tourism, and marine-based products often extend far beyond local communities, connecting coastal ecosystems to global markets. Ensuring that these supply chains are sustainable not only supports the protection of biodiversity within MPAs but also strengthens the economic viability of the Blue Economy. By creating direct connections between conservation outcomes and consumer choices, sustainable supply chains make MPAs integral to both ecological stewardship and responsible commerce.

Seafood supply chains provide one of the clearest opportunities for linking MPAs to sustainability. Overfishing and IUU fishing undermine marine conservation and the livelihoods of coastal communities. MPAs help replenish fish stocks by protecting spawning grounds and critical habitats, creating spillover benefits for adjacent fisheries. Certification schemes such as the Marine

Stewardship Council (MSC) or Fair Trade Fisheries highlight products sourced from areas that adhere to sustainable practices, including those adjacent to or influenced by MPAs. By supporting traceability systems that track seafood from ocean to consumer, MPAs can strengthen market confidence and reward fishers who comply with conservation regulations.

Traceability technologies play a key role in linking MPAs to sustainable supply chains. Blockchain systems, electronic monitoring, and vessel tracking ensure transparency in how marine resources are harvested and moved through supply networks. For example, blockchain can provide an immutable record of a fish's journey from a legal catch near an MPA to a retail outlet. This allows retailers and consumers to verify the sustainability of their purchases, creating market-driven incentives for compliance with MPA rules. Transparency also helps governments and businesses identify illegal activities that threaten both conservation and fair competition.

Tourism supply chains also benefit from connections to MPAs. Many MPAs are key attractions for diving, snorkeling, wildlife watching, and eco-tourism. By embedding sustainability standards into tourism supply chains—such as requiring eco-certified operators, sustainable accommodations, and environmentally responsible transport—MPAs can ensure that tourism revenues support conservation rather than contribute to degradation. Local communities benefit through employment and business opportunities, while visitors gain authentic and environmentally responsible experiences. Marketing that highlights MPAs as destinations of ecological importance further strengthens consumer awareness and demand for sustainable travel.

Marine-based products beyond seafood and tourism, such as pharmaceuticals, cosmetics, and seaweed-based goods, are also linked to supply chains that can be shaped by MPA management. Ensuring that these industries follow sustainable harvesting practices protects biodiversity while allowing continued innovation and production. Certification systems and benefit-sharing arrangements can ensure that communities living near MPAs receive fair compensation, creating economic incentives for long-term stewardship.

Linking MPAs to sustainable supply chains requires strong partnerships across sectors. Governments must provide regulatory frameworks and monitoring systems, businesses must commit to sustainability standards, and civil society must advocate for transparency and accountability. Consumer demand also plays a powerful role; as awareness grows, markets increasingly favor products and services tied to conservation.

By connecting conservation outcomes to global markets, MPAs become more than areas of protection—they become drivers of sustainable supply chains that reward responsible practices. This linkage ensures that the benefits of MPAs extend far beyond their boundaries, influencing the broader economy while reinforcing the ecological and social goals of marine conservation.

Cross-Sectoral Coordination

Cross-sectoral coordination is essential for the effective governance of oceans and the successful integration of MPAs within the Blue Economy. Oceans are used by multiple sectors—fisheries, shipping, tourism, energy, mining, and conservation—all of which often overlap in space and time. Without coordination, conflicting interests can lead to resource degradation, economic inefficiency, and social disputes. By fostering collaboration between different sectors, cross-sectoral coordination ensures that marine resources are managed holistically, balancing ecological protection with sustainable development.

At the heart of cross-sectoral coordination is the recognition that marine ecosystems and human activities are interconnected. For example, unsustainable fishing can deplete stocks critical to tourism, while shipping lanes may threaten sensitive habitats conserved within MPAs. Similarly, offshore energy development can conflict with fisheries or biodiversity conservation if poorly planned. Coordination mechanisms bring stakeholders together to identify overlaps, negotiate solutions, and create governance frameworks that minimize conflicts and enhance synergies.

MSP is one of the most effective tools for achieving cross-sectoral coordination. By allocating ocean space for different uses, MSP provides a structured process for balancing conservation and development. MPAs can be integrated into MSP frameworks to ensure that biodiversity and ecosystem services are protected alongside economic activities such as renewable energy, aquaculture, or transport. This approach reduces competition between sectors and promotes transparency in decision-making.

Institutional arrangements also play a critical role in facilitating coordination. Inter-agency committees, cross-sectoral working groups, and regional governance bodies provide platforms for collaboration. These institutions help align sectoral policies, clarify responsibilities, and avoid duplication of efforts. For instance, fisheries authorities, environmental agencies, and tourism departments can coordinate to develop management plans that recognize the interdependence of their sectors. Internationally, regional fisheries management organizations and transboundary marine commissions help neighboring countries align their policies, ensuring that ecosystems shared across borders are managed cooperatively.

Cross-sectoral coordination extends to data sharing and decision support. Many sectors collect valuable data on marine conditions, vessel traffic, resource use, or ecological status. Sharing this information across agencies and industries enables more accurate assessments of cumulative impacts and more effective management strategies. Digital platforms and decision support tools, such as GIS, facilitate integrated analyses that inform joint planning and monitoring.

Stakeholder engagement is another critical dimension. Effective coordination requires not only government and industry involvement but also the participation of local communities, NGOs, and indigenous peoples. These groups bring unique perspectives and traditional knowledge, ensuring that decisions are socially inclusive and grounded in local realities. By engaging multiple actors, coordination processes build trust, reduce conflicts, and enhance compliance with regulations.

Challenges to cross-sectoral coordination often arise from competing mandates, lack of communication, and resource constraints. However, when successful, coordination creates opportunities for synergy. For example, renewable energy projects can fund MPA monitoring, tourism operators can contribute to conservation awareness, and fisheries can benefit from spillover effects generated by protected areas.

Cross-sectoral coordination therefore serves as a cornerstone of effective marine governance. By aligning policies, reducing conflicts, and fostering collaboration, it ensures that MPAs are not isolated efforts but integrated elements of a broader system of sustainable ocean management. This collaborative approach strengthens both ecological outcomes and economic opportunities, advancing the goals of the Blue Economy.

Long-Term Strategic Vision and Targets

A long-term strategic vision and clear targets are essential for guiding the sustainable management of oceans and ensuring that MPAs achieve their full potential within the Blue Economy. Short-term projects or isolated interventions often fail to address the scale of environmental challenges or provide the consistency needed for ecological and social outcomes. By articulating a forward-looking vision and setting measurable, time-bound targets, governments and stakeholders create pathways for effective conservation, economic growth, and resilience that extend across generations.

At the heart of a long-term strategic vision is the recognition that ocean ecosystems are dynamic and interconnected. Management must therefore go beyond short-term fixes to embrace adaptive, ecosystem-based approaches that account for future environmental changes, including those driven by climate change. A strategic vision sets the overarching direction, establishing where societies want to be in terms of marine health, economic sustainability, and community resilience decades into the future. It provides coherence to policies, funding, and partnerships, ensuring that all efforts contribute toward common goals rather than fragmented actions.

Targets give substance to this vision by defining specific objectives and benchmarks against which progress can be measured. Global commitments, such as the Convention on Biological Diversity's "30x30" target to protect 30 percent of the ocean by 2030, exemplify how targets can drive momentum and accountability. For MPAs, targets may include not only the percentage of area protected but also measures of ecological effectiveness, such as improvements in biodiversity, fish biomass, or ecosystem services. Socio-economic targets are equally important, ensuring that communities benefit from conservation through sustainable fisheries, tourism, and climate resilience.

Developing a long-term vision requires broad participation. Governments, scientists, local communities, industries, and civil society must all contribute to defining priorities and strategies. Inclusive vision-setting processes ensure that goals are legitimate, equitable, and widely supported. This is especially important in regions where marine resources are central to livelihoods and cultural identity. Engaging stakeholders early also fosters ownership, increasing the likelihood that long-term targets are respected and achieved.

Monitoring and evaluation systems are critical for tracking progress toward strategic targets. Long-term data collection on ecological and socio-economic indicators allows managers to assess whether MPAs and related initiatives are delivering expected outcomes. Regular reviews provide opportunities to adjust strategies, ensuring that management remains responsive to changing conditions. Transparent reporting mechanisms also strengthen accountability, both domestically and within international frameworks.

A long-term vision also integrates financial sustainability. Strategic targets must be supported by reliable funding mechanisms, including public budgets, private investments, and innovative tools such as blue bonds and carbon credits. Securing financial stability ensures that MPAs and other conservation measures are not undermined by shifting political priorities or short-term funding cycles.

Importantly, long-term visions must align with broader international frameworks such as the Paris Agreement, the SDGs, and regional marine strategies. By linking local and national targets to global agendas, countries amplify their contributions and benefit from international cooperation, knowledge sharing, and funding opportunities.

Establishing a long-term strategic vision and targets transforms ocean governance from reactive management to proactive stewardship. By setting ambitious, measurable, and inclusive goals, societies can safeguard marine ecosystems, support resilient communities, and create a sustainable Blue Economy that endures for generations to come.

Chapter 9: Measuring Progress and Ensuring Accountability

The long-term success of MPAs and the Blue Economy depends on the ability to measure progress, demonstrate effectiveness, and uphold accountability. Without clear indicators, monitoring frameworks, and transparent reporting, MPAs risk becoming symbolic rather than impactful. This chapter examines the tools and systems used to evaluate performance, including ecological, socio-economic, governance, and financial indicators. It also explores global and regional reporting mechanisms, transparency in data sharing, and the role of adaptive management and policy reform. By ensuring accountability, these measures build trust, foster resilience, and secure lasting benefits for people and the planet.

Indicators for MPA Performance

Indicators for MPA performance are essential tools for measuring the effectiveness of conservation efforts and ensuring that MPAs deliver on their ecological, social, and economic objectives. Without clear indicators, MPAs risk becoming "paper parks" that exist in name but fail to achieve meaningful results. By defining and tracking measurable outcomes, indicators provide accountability, guide adaptive management, and demonstrate the value of MPAs within the broader Blue Economy framework.

Ecological indicators form the backbone of MPA performance evaluation. These indicators track changes in biodiversity, habitat health, and ecosystem processes. Common ecological measures include species abundance and diversity, fish biomass, coral reef cover, mangrove extent, and water quality. For example, increases in fish stocks within no-take zones serve as strong evidence of ecological recovery, while spillover into adjacent fisheries demonstrates benefits beyond MPA boundaries. Monitoring ecological indicators helps managers assess whether MPAs are meeting their core conservation objectives and adapt management strategies when outcomes fall short.

Socio-economic indicators are equally important, as MPAs affect the livelihoods, well-being, and cultural practices of local communities. Indicators may include household income from fisheries or tourism, food security levels, employment opportunities, and community perceptions of MPAs. Positive outcomes—such as increased tourism revenue or improved fish catches outside MPAs—help build public support for conservation. Social indicators such as stakeholder participation, equity in benefit-sharing, and respect for traditional rights also highlight the extent to which MPAs are inclusive and just. These measures ensure that conservation does not come at the expense of community resilience.

Governance indicators provide insights into the institutional and management effectiveness of MPAs. They track the strength of legal frameworks, enforcement capacity, monitoring systems, and stakeholder engagement. For instance, the presence of clear management plans, adequate staffing, and regular surveillance activities can serve as benchmarks of effective governance. Transparency, accountability, and conflict-resolution mechanisms are additional governance indicators that ensure MPAs are managed fairly and effectively. Strong governance not only supports compliance but also builds trust among stakeholders.

Financial indicators assess the sustainability of MPA funding. Effective MPAs require consistent resources for staffing, enforcement, monitoring, and community programs. Indicators may include the proportion of budgets covered by stable funding sources, revenue generated through tourism or payment for ecosystem services, and the diversity of funding mechanisms. Financial sustainability is critical to ensuring that conservation gains are not lost due to economic or political shifts.

Adaptive management relies on integrating these different types of indicators into a comprehensive framework. By monitoring ecological, socio-economic, governance, and financial indicators together, managers can assess trade-offs, identify synergies, and adjust strategies in real time. For example, if ecological indicators show improvement but socio-economic indicators reveal community dissatisfaction, managers may need to adjust zoning or develop alternative livelihood programs.

International frameworks such as the IUCN Green List of Protected and Conserved Areas and the Marine Protected Area Management Effectiveness (MPAME) framework provide standardized sets of indicators that countries can adapt to local contexts. Using such frameworks ensures comparability across regions and contributes to global assessments of marine conservation progress.

Indicators for MPA performance are therefore much more than technical measures; they are the foundation of accountability, transparency, and adaptive management. By tracking outcomes across ecological, social, governance, and financial dimensions, indicators ensure that MPAs fulfill their promise as vital tools for biodiversity conservation, climate resilience, and sustainable development within the Blue Economy.

Monitoring and Evaluation Frameworks

Monitoring and evaluation (M&E) frameworks are critical for ensuring that MPAs achieve their intended objectives and continue to deliver ecological, social, and economic benefits. These frameworks provide structured approaches to track progress, assess outcomes, and inform adaptive management. In the context of the Blue Economy, where conservation must coexist with development, robust M&E systems are essential for demonstrating the effectiveness of MPAs, maintaining accountability, and securing long-term support from governments, communities, and international partners.

Monitoring refers to the systematic collection of data over time to track changes in ecosystems, human activities, and governance processes. Evaluation, on the other hand, assesses the significance of those changes in relation to the objectives of an MPA. Together, monitoring and evaluation create feedback loops that allow managers to learn from experience, identify challenges, and refine strategies to enhance performance.

Ecological monitoring is a central component of M&E frameworks. It involves tracking biodiversity, habitat health, and ecosystem services. For example, indicators such as fish biomass, coral reef cover, mangrove extent, or water quality are monitored regularly to measure whether conservation objectives are being met. Long-term ecological datasets help identify trends, assess resilience to climate change, and evaluate the impact of management measures such as no-take zones. These insights are essential for ensuring that MPAs deliver tangible biodiversity benefits.

Socio-economic monitoring complements ecological assessments by evaluating the impacts of MPAs on people. This includes tracking income from fisheries and tourism, food security, employment opportunities, and community well-being. Evaluation goes further by examining whether MPAs are contributing to poverty reduction, livelihood diversification, and equitable benefit-sharing. Social dimensions such as stakeholder participation, gender inclusion, and respect for traditional rights are also critical to ensuring that MPAs are fair and widely supported.

Governance monitoring focuses on institutional arrangements, legal frameworks, enforcement mechanisms, and stakeholder engagement. Evaluating governance performance ensures that MPAs are not only legally established but also effectively managed. Key metrics might include the existence of management plans, adequacy of staff and funding, enforcement efficiency, and transparency in decision-making. Strong governance monitoring builds accountability and helps identify areas where capacity building or institutional reforms are needed.

Financial monitoring is another important dimension, given that many MPAs struggle with insufficient funding. Tracking financial indicators such as revenue from tourism, grants, or innovative financing mechanisms (e.g., blue bonds or carbon credits) allows managers to evaluate whether MPAs have sustainable funding streams. Evaluation helps determine whether financial resources are being used efficiently and equitably, ensuring that conservation outcomes are not undermined by budgetary shortfalls.

Effective M&E frameworks rely on clear objectives, measurable indicators, and participatory processes. Engaging stakeholders in monitoring builds trust, incorporates local knowledge, and ensures that outcomes are relevant to community needs. Advances in technology—such as remote sensing, mobile applications, and automated data platforms—are increasingly integrated into M&E, making monitoring more cost-effective and accessible.

International initiatives such as the MPAME framework and the IUCN Green List provide standardized approaches that countries can adapt to their contexts. These frameworks enable comparisons across regions and contribute to global assessments of progress toward biodiversity and climate goals.

Monitoring and evaluation frameworks are not static; they must evolve as conditions change. By embedding adaptive learning into governance, M&E ensures that MPAs remain resilient, effective, and aligned with both conservation priorities and the sustainable development objectives of the Blue Economy.

Transparency and Data Sharing

Transparency and data sharing are vital components of effective MPA management and the broader governance of the Blue Economy. Oceans are shared resources that span jurisdictions and support diverse stakeholders, from local communities and national governments to international organizations and private industries. Effective governance therefore depends on open access to information, accountability in decision-making, and collaboration built on trust. Transparency ensures that policies and practices are visible and accountable, while data sharing enables the collective use

98

of knowledge for more informed, equitable, and sustainable outcomes.

In the context of MPAs, transparency begins with clear communication of objectives, regulations, and management decisions. Communities and industries affected by MPAs need to understand the rules governing access and use, as well as the evidence that supports them. When decision-making processes are transparent, stakeholders are more likely to perceive MPAs as legitimate and to comply with regulations. Transparent governance also strengthens accountability by allowing external actors—such as civil society groups, NGOs, and researchers—to monitor whether governments and institutions are meeting their commitments.

Data sharing builds on transparency by making scientific, ecological, and socio-economic information widely accessible. Oceans generate vast datasets from satellite systems, ecological surveys, vessel tracking, and community monitoring. Sharing these data across institutions, sectors, and borders enhances coordination and reduces duplication of effort. For example, vessel movement data from AIS can be shared between fisheries authorities, conservation agencies, and international organizations to detect IUU fishing. Similarly, ecological data on coral reef health or fish populations can be shared among scientists, managers, and communities to guide adaptive management.

Technological innovations are expanding opportunities for transparency and data sharing. Online platforms and open-access databases provide real-time information on marine activities and environmental conditions. Initiatives such as Global Fishing Watch allow the public to track fishing vessels worldwide, empowering NGOs, journalists, and citizens to hold actors accountable. Cloud-based platforms and digital dashboards enable managers and stakeholders to visualize data, monitor trends, and evaluate performance collaboratively. These tools not only improve decision-making but also democratize access to information, making ocean governance more inclusive.

Data sharing is equally important for building trust and cooperation across scales. Local communities contribute valuable knowledge through participatory monitoring, while scientists provide technical expertise, and governments establish policy frameworks. Sharing data ensures that these different knowledge systems inform one another, creating stronger and more holistic management strategies. It also allows countries to coordinate across borders, an essential aspect of conserving migratory species and managing transboundary ecosystems.

Challenges remain, particularly around data ownership, confidentiality, and capacity. Governments or industries may withhold information for political or competitive reasons, while communities may be excluded due to lack of access to technology. Addressing these challenges requires clear protocols on data governance, capacity-building initiatives to empower local actors, and international agreements that set standards for open data practices.

Embedding transparency and data sharing into MPA management strengthens accountability, fosters cooperation, and enhances adaptive learning. By ensuring that information is accessible and decisions are open to scrutiny, these practices build trust among stakeholders and align conservation with democratic principles. In the Blue Economy, where sustainability depends on collective responsibility, transparency and data sharing are indispensable for ensuring that marine resources are managed fairly and effectively.

Adaptive Management and Policy Reform

Adaptive management and policy reform are essential strategies for ensuring that MPAs remain effective in the face of changing ecological, social, and economic conditions. Oceans are dynamic systems, influenced by climate change, shifting species distributions, technological advances, and evolving human needs. Static policies and rigid management structures cannot adequately respond to these challenges. Adaptive management provides a flexible, iterative approach to governance, while policy reform creates the legal and institutional foundations needed to embed adaptability into marine conservation and the wider Blue Economy.

Adaptive management is based on the principle of "learning by doing." Managers set objectives, implement actions, monitor outcomes, and adjust strategies based on what works and what does not. In MPAs, this process allows for continuous improvement in protecting biodiversity, sustaining fisheries, and supporting community livelihoods. For example, if monitoring shows that a no-take zone is not achieving recovery of fish populations, managers may revise zoning, adjust enforcement, or implement complementary measures such as habitat restoration. This iterative cycle ensures that conservation efforts are not undermined by unforeseen ecological changes or management failures.

Policy reform is critical to institutionalizing adaptive management. Many MPA systems are constrained by outdated laws, fragmented responsibilities, or limited capacity for enforcement. Reforming policies to explicitly include adaptive management principles ensures that governance frameworks are responsive and resilient. For instance, policies can mandate regular performance evaluations, require the integration of climate science into management, or provide mechanisms for stakeholder participation in decision-making. Such reforms make adaptability not just an option but a core requirement of marine governance.

Climate change is a key driver of the need for adaptive management and policy reform. Rising sea temperatures, ocean acidification, and sea level rise alter ecosystems in ways that cannot be fully predicted. MPAs must therefore be designed and managed with flexibility to accommodate shifting baselines. This includes identifying and protecting climate refugia, adjusting boundaries to account for species migrations, and integrating MPAs into larger networks that provide ecological connectivity. Policy frameworks that anticipate climate impacts and allow for dynamic adjustments ensure that MPAs remain relevant and effective under future conditions.

Stakeholder engagement is another vital aspect of adaptive management. Communities, industries, and civil society must be involved in shaping policies and management decisions. Their participation ensures that conservation strategies are locally appropriate, socially just, and more likely to succeed. Policy reform can strengthen stakeholder involvement by establishing co-management structures, ensuring equity in decision-making, and recognizing traditional and indigenous knowledge. This inclusivity builds trust and enhances compliance, making adaptive management more effective.

Adaptive management also requires robust monitoring and evaluation systems to provide the evidence base for decision-making. Policies must support investment in data collection, scientific research, and technological innovation. Access to reliable information allows managers to detect trends, test new approaches, and respond rapidly to emerging challenges.

By combining adaptive management with policy reform, MPAs can evolve alongside changing environmental and social realities. This dual approach ensures that conservation remains effective, resilient, and aligned with the principles of the Blue Economy. Flexible governance that learns from experience, incorporates science, and responds to community needs is the foundation of long-term marine sustainability.

Global and Regional Reporting Mechanisms

Global and regional reporting mechanisms play a vital role in tracking the effectiveness of MPAs and ensuring accountability in ocean governance. These mechanisms provide structured processes for collecting, analyzing, and sharing information on the status of marine ecosystems, conservation progress, and the implementation of international commitments. By linking local and national MPA management to global frameworks, reporting mechanisms strengthen transparency, foster collaboration, and help align efforts across scales in support of the Blue Economy.

At the global level, several frameworks provide reporting mechanisms that track progress in marine conservation. The CBD is one of the most prominent, requiring countries to submit National Biodiversity Strategies and Action Plans (NBSAPs) and periodic reports on their achievements. Through the CBD's post-2020 Global Biodiversity Framework, targets such as protecting 30 percent of the world's oceans by 2030 ("30x30") are monitored using standardized reporting indicators. MPAs are a key component of these reports, and national submissions feed into global assessments of biodiversity trends.

The United Nations Framework Convention on Climate Change (UNFCCC) also provides a platform for reporting linkages between marine ecosystems and climate policy. Nationally Determined Contributions (NDCs) often include commitments to protect blue carbon ecosystems such as mangroves and seagrasses. By reporting these measures through the UNFCCC, countries demonstrate how MPAs contribute to both climate mitigation and adaptation goals. This integration strengthens the visibility of marine conservation within global climate governance.

The SDGs framework provides another layer of global reporting. Specifically, SDG 14 ("Life Below Water") tracks progress on marine conservation, fisheries management, and sustainable resource use. Indicators under SDG 14 require countries to report on the coverage and effectiveness of MPAs, offering a comprehensive picture of how marine conservation supports sustainable development. By aligning national reports with SDG indicators, countries contribute to a shared global database that informs policymakers, researchers, and the public.

At the regional level, reporting mechanisms are often tailored to specific ecological or political contexts. Regional Seas Conventions, coordinated by the United Nations Environment Programme (UNEP), provide platforms for neighboring countries to collaborate on marine conservation and report on shared ecosystems. Examples include the Barcelona Convention in the Mediterranean and the Nairobi Convention in the Western Indian Ocean. These mechanisms facilitate coordinated reporting on MPAs, pollution control, and habitat protection, ensuring that conservation extends beyond national borders to address transboundary challenges.

Regional Fisheries Management Organizations (RFMOs) also contribute by reporting on the status of fish stocks and the effectiveness of spatial measures such as no-take zones or seasonal closures. Their work provides essential data for integrating fisheries management with MPA networks, particularly in areas beyond national jurisdiction.

Global and regional reporting mechanisms face challenges, including inconsistent data collection, limited capacity in developing countries, and variations in reporting standards. Efforts to harmonize methodologies, build technical capacity, and provide financial support are critical for improving accuracy and comparability. Open-access platforms and digital tools are increasingly used to streamline reporting and make information widely available, enhancing transparency and accountability.

By linking local conservation outcomes to international frameworks, global and regional reporting mechanisms ensure that MPAs are not managed in isolation but are part of a coherent global strategy. They create accountability, mobilize resources, and foster cooperation, ensuring that progress in marine protection contributes meaningfully to global biodiversity, climate, and sustainable development goals.

Conclusion

The Blue Economy and MPAs represent two interwoven strategies that together provide a pathway toward sustainable ocean governance. As global pressures on marine ecosystems intensify, from climate change and overfishing to pollution and coastal development, these approaches highlight the importance of aligning conservation with development to secure both ecological integrity and human well-being. The chapters explored throughout this work illustrate the breadth and depth of opportunities and challenges in integrating MPAs within the framework of the Blue Economy, underscoring the critical need for long-term, adaptive, and inclusive approaches.

At the heart of the Blue Economy is the recognition that oceans are not only sources of biodiversity but also engines of economic activity and cultural identity. Harnessing this potential requires careful stewardship that maintains the health of ecosystems while supporting the livelihoods of millions of people. MPAs provide a cornerstone for achieving this balance by protecting critical habitats, sustaining fisheries, conserving biodiversity, and supporting resilience against climate impacts. When linked to sustainable supply chains, innovative financing, and cross-sectoral coordination, MPAs serve as both ecological sanctuaries and drivers of economic opportunity.

The examination of governance frameworks highlights the need for strong legal, institutional, and participatory structures to ensure MPA effectiveness. International agreements, national policies, and regional cooperation create the scaffolding through which MPAs contribute to global biodiversity and climate targets. Meanwhile, stakeholder engagement, community co-management, and cultural inclusion ensure that conservation strategies are not imposed from above but co-created with those who depend on the ocean most directly. The importance of transparent governance, supported by reliable monitoring and evaluation frameworks, further reinforces accountability and builds trust among diverse actors.

Technological innovation has emerged as a powerful enabler of effective MPA management. Advances in satellite monitoring, artificial intelligence, blockchain, and environmental DNA are transforming the ways in which ecosystems are studied, illegal activities are deterred, and sustainable practices are rewarded. These tools make it possible to scale up protection efforts, enhance enforcement, and integrate data across multiple sectors. At the same time, they must be coupled with equitable access and capacity-building to ensure that all communities can benefit from technological progress.

Climate change remains the defining challenge of our era, and MPAs are increasingly recognized as vital tools for both adaptation and mitigation. Protecting blue carbon ecosystems, strengthening ecological resilience, and enhancing the adaptive capacity of coastal communities ensures that MPAs contribute directly to climate solutions. The ocean–climate nexus reinforces the interconnectedness of these agendas, demonstrating that protecting marine ecosystems is inseparable from addressing the global climate crisis.

The path forward requires ambition, cooperation, and commitment. Long-term strategic visions, measurable targets, and sustained financing are essential for scaling up and sustaining MPA networks. Equally, policy reform and adaptive management must remain central to governance, ensuring that MPAs can evolve with changing ecological and social realities. By embedding MPAs within the broader Blue Economy, societies can unlock synergies that deliver prosperity, equity, and resilience.

The story of MPAs within the Blue Economy is one of opportunity: the opportunity to protect life below water while sustaining life above it, the opportunity to align local needs with global goals, and the opportunity to demonstrate that economic development and environmental stewardship are not mutually exclusive. By seizing these opportunities, the international community can chart a course toward oceans that are healthier, economies that are more sustainable, and societies that are better prepared for the challenges and possibilities of the future.